THIS IS WAR

By Apostle Lynne Schulze

outskirts
press

Dedication

I would like to dedicate this book to my Lord and Savior! My refuge and strong tower! You have consistently loved me, even when I was your enemy, and for that I am eternally grateful. I did what you told me to do by writing this book. Victory is the outcome! My confidence is in you. I pray that you are glorified in these pages, and your Spirit moves on your people as they consume its contents. Let your anointing run through the pages, and transfer your fire into their spirit, that they would declare war on the enemy in his own camp, and take it to him! Destroying mindsets, philosophies, old strategies and demolishing every plot and plan in the Devil's cauldron!

Thank you; Lord, for your love and mercy that you extend to me daily! For blessing me with my husband, Apostle Curt Schulze, who sees me on the inside, my true love, who pushes me to "go and be powerful" when I feel powerless! Thank you, Lord, for my mom "Regina "(who's there with you, in the beauty of you holiness, worshipping)! I love and miss you mom, but our reunion will be eternal! Mr. Bill, who will win this war! My dad, Pastors Ben and Gloria, who prayed for me, and all of my children and grandchildren who are soldiers gearing up for battle! Thank you for my sisters and brothers; we are one in the Spirit, covered by the "blood of Jesus"! For our congregation, FCM, that is filled with "warriors" who will devour the enemy, stay on the offense, strike a fatal blow into the second Heaven. For family and friends, I love you all, and I thank you for your support in writing this book!

Now, to the "body of Christ': the battle is raging, let's strap in, because this is **WAR**!!!

Table of Contents

Introduction

The Lord is a man of war

One of my favorite scriptures is, "The Lord is a man of war; the Lord is his name" (Exodus 15:3). There are so many faces to God, but this one always stands out to me. The Lord, our God the commander in chief, the general of generals!

We know that Moses wrote this scripture inspired by the Holy Spirit. It was in reference to the showdown at the Red Sea, where Pharaoh's army pursued the people of God and the Lord showed up and showed out, as they say.

Imagine, this truly must have been a sight to see. The Lord using his creation, the waters, to destroy his enemy! Truly, his weapons are not carnal!

"And with the blast of thy nostrils the waters were gathered together, the floods stood upright as a heap, and the depths were congealed in the heart of the sea" (Exodus 15:8).

Here we see the Lord God Almighty making war with his enemy using weapons of his choosing and fighting a battle for his people. All the while, man has his part in the confrontation, but it is the Lord who gives the strategy, who guides by his staff, instructs the believer, and wins the battle. That is our position in our journey as believers in Jesus Christ! We are led by his Spirit, but he truly is swinging the ax!

This is war!!

1

Open our eyes!

^{15} *And when the servant of the man of God was risen early, and gone forth, behold, a host compassed the city both with horses and chariots. And his servant said unto him, Alas, my master! How shall we do?* ^{16} *And he answered, Fear not: for they that be with us are more than they that be with them.* ^{17} *And Elisha prayed, and said, Lord, I pray thee; open his eyes that he may see. And the Lord opened the eyes of the young man; and he saw: and, behold, the mountain was full of horses and chariots of fire round about Elisha (2 Kings 6:15-17).*

I have a question for you. How often, in your lifetime have you acknowledged, confronted or addressed your surroundings? I know this question makes no sense to many, is not worded properly, and seems extraneous. Address my surroundings?

Years ago, I remember watching a 60 Minute episode where law enforcement had to enter a room, pass through it, and recall to their instructor everything that was in the room!

On many occasions, they would remember the flowerpot, the poster on the wall, the couch and chair, but inevitably, never see the gunman in the corner, pointing a gun right at them!!

This is what I think of when I think about the Spirit realm. There's so much going on around us, yet we are not cognizant.

We pray to a God that we do not see; yet we believe. While at the same time, not ignoring that his throne resides in another realm, the realm of the Spirit!!

The Word of God reminds us that God is a spirit; therefore, we must worship him in Spirit and in truth (John 4:23). This is a hard scripture to comprehend when we tend to only see what's right in front of us.

What is a realm? The definition is "a kingdom, kingly reign or a field or domain of activity!" Within this realm are various dimensions. Dimensions are just a measurable part of that realm--length, height and width. For instance, looking into the Spirit realm, you could see angels, demons, rulers, thrones, principalities and the sort. But the dimension might be from the surface of the earth reaching to the stars only, and no higher than the stars, or looking through an opening of a vortex or portal the size of a square box in length, depth and width!

Now, with that being said, imagine all around and through the earth, as you know it, is an entire kingdom, that reaches beyond the stars, that functions with our Father on the throne, King Jesus at his right hand, angels, rulers, celestials of all kinds, with a governmental order in place! The same as here on the earth, but different! With the earth being the natural, but the Spirit realm being the SUPER natural!

Let's look at scripture.

"Not all flesh is the same: Men have one kind of flesh, animals have another, birds another, and fish another. There are also heavenly bodies and earthly bodies. But the splendor of the heavenly bodies is of one degree and the splendor of the earthly bodies is of another. The sun has one degree of splendor, the moon another, and the stars another; and star differs from star in splendor" (1Cor15: 39-40)!

The one thing that really stands firm is the fact that our God is truly a creator. There are various kinds of bugs, ants, roaches, birds, animals and people here on earth, yet the same diversity in the heavenlies!

The earth mimics the kingdom of God, in its fashion, because the creator is the same. *In the beginning, God created the heaven and the earth (Genesis 1: 1).*

Remember, *the Earth is the Lord's, the fullness thereof; the world, and they that dwell therein (Psalms 24:1)!!!* It all belongs to him!

My question to you is: have you checked out your surroundings lately?

As I write this book right now, I have an angel standing on each side of me. The angel on the left has his hand on my shoulder; the one on the right is standing firm. Above me one is moving in a circular motion as if he's worshipping the Lord, while my music is playing "Psalm 23", by Shane & Shane. This very moment is so surreal.

There's a Spirit realm all around you, and there's a war going on!

2

Thy Kingdom Come!

Thy Kingdom come. Thy will be done in earth, as it is in heaven (Matthew 6:10).

Every time I hear this scripture, something rises in me! The power in the word alone moves me! It paints a picture, displays an image. What an Imagination! God designed your imagination! The Hebrew word for imagination is (Yatsar) meaning to form or squeeze into shape, to make or mold like a potter, to fashion or frame.

The Lord told me, "Lynne, this is how I made you! Before I formed you in the belly, I knew you (Jeremiah 1).

The word Knew means, "to ascertain by seeing." In Genesis 11: 6, the people on the earth were trying to build a tower to Heaven. When God came down to take a look at what they were doing (which was an evil thing) he said, "and now nothing will be restrained from them which they have imagined to do." He attributed their progress to the imagination! The imagination is a creative source within.

Wow, imagine that!

In the spirit realm, the Lord will show you forms and images, places and things, like a picture show. In my relationship with the Lord, he will show me talking to someone, or praying for someone, and I know, and I have learned this is what he wants me to do concerning this person, place or thing!

Ok, now let's take a look at the Kingdom of God. Let's imagine and consider the King's domain!

Thy Kingdom is an everlasting Kingdom, and thy dominion endureth throughout all generations (Psalms 145:13).

When I picture this Kingdom, it would be nothing without a King! That's what makes it a Kingdom!

For those who believe in the Father, Son and the Holy Spirit, this is paramount. We believe and know, one day we will be with our Lord in his kingdom, so we prepare here on earth!

In the Spirit realm, everybody knows who's Lord. No one is trying to figure out who's in charge!!

Here on earth, it's a faith walk! You pray to a God that you cannot see; yet you believe! That takes faith!! But do we really "not see him"?

I pose this scenario to you. In looking at our creator, take note of all that he has done. Look up at the sky, that expanse, look at the vastness!

You can see the sky over every city, country, and nation you travel to, and the stars you see are innumerable! The sun is like clockwork and stays in place. There is a moon, which only comes out at night in most parts of the world, the sphere of our universe!

Trees that breathe. And gravity--what goes up must come down, unless you're in space! What a creator, and there's more! How babies are formed in the womb, why your heart keeps beating all night long, how your body can heal itself and I can go on and on and on! All the while, scientists are still discovering what the Lord has already done!

When you think about the design of it all, it makes you realize the designer must be astounding!

"For the invisible things of him from the creation of the world are clearly seen, being understood by the things that are made, even his eternal power and Godhead; so that they are without excuse" (Romans 1:20).

It is almost like the Lord is saying, "I exist, and I can show you better than I can tell you. The invisible made the visible!"

There are other ways the invisible affects the visible, or the supernatural affects the natural.

In the scriptures, after Jesus went into Galilee and proclaimed (preached) the gospel (good news)

"The time is fulfilled," He said, "and the kingdom of God is near. Repent and believe in the gospel" (Mark 1:15).

He made the people aware, (or warned the people) to repent because God's kingdom, with him being the king, was near or standing right in front of them! He was letting them know, with the kingdom of God so close, you must repent and reconcile with the king!

Another scripture, one of my favorites, explains how things work in this domain of the King!

"But if I drive out demons by the finger of God,

then the kingdom of God has come upon you" (Luke 11:20).

When demons are expelled, driven out of a person, place or thing, it is because the Kingdom came upon (as in touching) that thing, place or person!

When Moses was sent to Pharaoh by God to tell him, "Let my people go," the magicians, said, "this is the finger of God." They were referring to all of the plagues that the Lord had sent to destroy Egypt!

They referenced his finger!! He touched with his finger and destruction came!!

This is such a powerful piece of revelation!

Because of the power that's in this invisible Kingdom of our God, one touch and things that were hidden can be exposed and dealt with!

When something is hidden from the natural eye, the light in the kingdom can expose what's hidden with one touch!! Wherever the King is, his domain is with him!

Look at the scripture!

Heal the sick in that town and say to them,"The kingdom of God has come upon you" (Luke 10:9).

The Lord told his disciples to heal the sick, and when you do, let them know that the healing came from the Kingdom that came upon (as in touching) you!

Once again, because of the power that's in this invisible Kingdom of God, one touch and healing was provided!! Now you see the fruit of what God's invisible power can do.

This is the Kingdom of our God! It exuberates his power!!

Power to win wars!!!

3

Where is this Kingdom?

Let's look at Luke 17:20-21;

²⁰ And when he was demanded of the Pharisees, when the kingdom of God should come, he answered them and said, the kingdom of God cometh not with observation:

²¹ Neither shall they say, Lo here! Or, lo there! For, behold, the kingdom of God is within you.

They will not say, it is over here, or it's over there.

For behold (to see with attention) the Kingdom of God is within you!!!!

When our Lord and Savior walked the earth, He was the King of the Kingdom of Heaven! This is why Jesus would say, the kingdom is at hand, meaning, nearby, because he was present! Wherever Jesus Christ, the king is, so is his kingdom (Matthew 4:17)!

Today, many are waiting for the full manifestation of the Kingdom of God to come here and be set up on earth, where Christ, after his return, will rule over the nations of this planet (Revelation 21:21). But until he returns, we are citizens of the Kingdom of Heaven, representing our King here on earth! We have been, "Born Again" so our birth certificate is registered in Heaven (Philippians 3:21).

Now, at this very moment, we are seated with Christ!

Ephesians 2:6 "...*and hath raised us up together and made us sit together in heavenly places in Christ Jesus."*

This is our position in the spirit realm; we are "in Christ Jesus "if we would just believe the Word!

Also, Christ is in us as well, the only hope of glory (Colossians 1:27).

The Lord has instructed us, *to heal the sick herein, and say unto them, "The kingdom of God is come nigh unto you" (Luke 10:9)!*

What is the Lord saying? The supernatural, almighty, healer, deliverer, redeemer is on the inside of you. Remember, where the King is, so is his Kingdom! In the "Spirit Realm" this is how you are known!

Your understanding of this revelation will catapult you to higher dimensions. This is why we have authority, Christ who lives in us, gives us the keys to the kingdom!

Whatsoever you bind on earth will be bound in Heaven, and whatsoever you loose on earth shall be loosed in Heaven (Matthew 16:19)!

This is a key to tie a devil up, not allow him to function, or command him to loose what he has in bondage!

There are portals that allow demons to travel to and from the spirit realm to our natural realm. In the Spirit realm, the Lord has shown me portals and told me to close them! With the authority in the name of Jesus, I would command it to close, and the portal would close!

I can hear the naysayers now!

"Demons? No way, some of you Christians are just too deep!"

I know this sounds like a science fiction movie, but most of the ideas a lot of dark, movies are projecting are coming from a thought generated by some kind of demon promoting the kingdom of darkness! We are just so oblivious to some of the enemy's tactics!

Personally, I am bewildered; so many don't believe these demons actually exist!! The Bible says, that Jesus was manifest into the earth to destroy the works of the enemy (1John 3:8). What enemy? The one that you can't see, that you don't believe exists! The Devil and his cronies operating from the realm of the spirit!

The scripture teaches, *"You wrestle (a violent and intense struggle) not against flesh and blood" (Ephesians 6:12).* You are in the fight whether you believe it or not! It would behoove you to know how to fight, and what weapons are at your disposal. You are contending with an enemy that you do not see.

What kind of bullets do you use on an "invisible thief"? **This is war**!

The Lord has given us the authority to forbid or allow whatsoever you "put in bonds" or tie up as well as whatsoever you loosen or break free, dissolve or melt! This is a standing principle in the Word of God that should not be ignored. Knowing this has been a life-changer to many!

Remember, since the King lives in us his authority must live in us as well!

Stop looking for God to show up somewhere else! A conference, a convention on the other side of town. The Lord and his Kingdom are right here with you, within you!!

Now, Go, and be powerful, there's a war going on!!

4

Why Daddy Why?

My birth name is Lynne Heflin. I was born in 1962 in Washington DC. I have four sisters and four brothers. I grew up in DC until I was six years old, then moved to rural Virginia on a 400-acre farm with my grandparents. Sister and Daddy Henry, as they were affectionately known, were people of great character! Everyone knew them as being selfless, kindhearted, generous and loving, all wrapped up into one!

My grandparents raised me and my siblings and some cousins, grandbabies, a friend's child and everyone else's kids as well! They would give their last for you and expected nothing in return! They are both with the Lord now, but the older I get, the more my love for them grows. They gave their all, for all!

We had chickens, pigs, horses, a cow, and lots of dogs! We lived off the land. There was corn, beans, peas, tomatoes, potatoes, collards--you name it, and we produced it!

There was seedtime and harvest time!

Just to give you a little about my background.

My grandfather was my mentor! He taught me how to drive a tractor, haul wood, dig up potatoes with a hoe, draw water from the well, and all aspects of farm life.

At the age of nine, I used to ride my bike to what we called the "backfield." The "backfield" was just valley after valley of grass, arrayed with the smell of honey-suckle and wild strawberries, lined with the sound of crickets, bees, and beetle bugs.

When I reached the backfield, (there were two fields before this one) I would lie down on the grass and look up at the sky mesmerized by the look and shape of the clouds. I would talk to God!

I asked him where he was, "Are you in the clouds, how did you make all of this--sun, sky, grass, flowers? I didn't know why I had all these questions, or why I would wait until I got to the backfield to talk to God!

To my grandfather I was known for saying, "Why daddy, why?" I wanted to know how things came to be, and what was the reason and purpose for a thing, and why do we do things a certain way. I would drive him crazy with this rhetorical question, "Why daddy, why?" Later in life, I would ask my father in Heaven the same question, Why daddy why? Hardly realizing it, eventually I would start to get some answers to my exasperating questions.

My life has been complicated at best, but God has sustained me. I have come to discover that most fami-lies are dysfunctional, blended, added to, stirred up and compromised, but all coming from one blood, that being of Adam!

I accepted Jesus Christ as my savior at the age of 18,

and stumbled and fell and crawled, and ran, and tip-toed, and blundered, until I decided to stop running, repent and receive him as Lord over my life!

When I was 22 years old, I told the Lord I wanted to see him. I didn't know the Bible, and I really wasn't aware of what I was asking, I just wanted to see my God (the one I would talk to in the backfield)!

One night, while lying in my bed, the Lord came to me. I was prompted by the Holy Spirit to wake up, so I did! I didn't know the Holy Spirit back then. I just thought I woke up for no reason. I assumed I just couldn't sleep!

I lived on the third floor, and the apartment that I lived in had windows that went to the floor. Outside of the window, there was a courtyard that was filled with trees. There were trails and pathways that ran between the trees.

As I sat up in my bed, I saw a light begin to manifest at the foot of the bed! It grew in size until it was so blinding, I couldn't see! The light illuminated out of my window, into the courtyard of my apartment building, I watched it just fill the room and the outside atmosphere! I wondered, could anyone else see what was happening? This is beyond comprehension! I could not grasp what was happening in the moment.

My heart froze in place, fear overtook me, and I couldn't move! I looked out the window and around my bedroom and the entire courtyard filled with trees was lit up!! I still could not move. I heard the Lord say to me, "I am the Lord, do not be afraid!"

We spoke to each other, and I never moved my lips! I didn't understand how this conversation was taking place! I was a baby Christian, with very little under-standing of the Spirit world. I could not believe he was there and talking to me!! Why, daddy, why?

I knew no one would believe me, because I couldn't believe me!! Yet it was happening right before my eyes! I told the Lord I wanted to see him, and he showed up. As a new believer in Christ, this increased my faith im-mensely; I have seen the Lord Jesus! After my encoun-ter with the Lord, I realized I would never be the same. Jesus is real! Now, I wanted more!

Knowing who your "daddy" is in wartime can be crucial!

5

Don't be afraid of the Dark!

When someone says darkness to me, I tend to think in a spiritual context first.

It's hard to see when it's dark outside. If it were not for the streetlights or the moon, it would be hard to see where you are going.

Born in Washington D.C. In 1962, I lived in the city until the age of six years old. We jumped double-dutch and played jacks on the front steps, I don't remember much about my life before then. But where we lived, we had streetlights. When the lights came on, you had to be in the house.

At an early age, we have all learned light will brighten dark places!

On April 4, 1968 Dr. Martin Luther King Jr. was assassinated while carrying out the plan of the Lord for his life. Riots broke out in the nation's Capital! There was arson and loitering, gunfire and utter chaos! Twelve people were killed, 1097 injured, 6100 arrested! The destruction of the riots caused 25 million dollars' worth of damage! Such a dark time in

American history!

Where we lived became dangerous to stay, so we moved to Partlow, Virginia on our grandparents' farm.

This was the country!

This was a 400-acre farm, with livestock, no running water, and no indoor plumbing. When nightfall came, it was dark! What I call, beyond blackness.

You couldn't see your hand in front of you! You knew your hand was there, but you couldn't see it!

That's what dealing in darkness is like. You are very much aware of things, but you can't see! Still, there's a presence!

The Lord was explaining darkness to me. He advised me there were characteristics to darkness. Darkness has a personality!

It has a presence!! A personality is a combination of characteristics.

When darkness is in the room: obscurity, uncertainty, the unknown is evident. Darkness covers up what's present!

There's presence in darkness.

Notice in a dark room, if a small stream of light penetrates, you will see shadows in the room in various places. A shadow can only be produced when light hits an object and reveals its presence. Light is a revealer!

Let's look at Genesis 1:2-3

"And the earth was without form, and void; and darkness was upon the face of the deep. And the Spirit of God moved upon the face of the waters. And God said let there be light: and there was light."

Here we see God, the creator, doing what he does

best--creating. He said, let there be light, and light came. But let's look at another scripture that brings even more clarity.

"For God, who commanded the light to shine (to beam) out of darkness, hath shined in our hearts..." 2 Corinthians 4:6.

Here, Paul is referencing Genesis 1:2-3, but giving more insight. The Light shone out of the darkness, which means, when the light came, it manifest (or beamed, radiated out of) the darkness.

Jesus is the Light! The Light of Christ expels darkness, forces it out and away, like an explosion!

Another meaning for darkness would be ignorance. So many believers are in darkness (ignorance) because they have very little light or not much of Christ in their lives.

We tend to fear what we can't see! We reach out in darkness trying to feel our way through, quoting scriptures, "God does not give me the spirit of fear..." and calling this faith! We may be speaking the word with no authority or expectation, yet there's no time invested, so we get very few results.

The remedy is to read the Word of God and meditate on his word; thus, turning the light on!

God's word is a lamp unto my feet, a light unto my path! The Word is the light! The Word, (your Bible) will expose the dark things in our lives. Once the Word exposes where the enemy is hiding, you can declare war and get the victory!

I declare war!!!

6

Attention, Soldier!!

Not being aware of the Spirit realm or your adversary, the Devil, demons, evil spirits or just God's host of angels to aid you, leaves you helpless concerning spiritual warfare!

So many believers are not aware of the fight that they are in, and the weapons God has provided for the battle.

There is so much unfamiliarity in the Body of Christ concerning spiritual things and the influence of demonic spirits. When the battle is raging, many don't recognize where the fight is coming from and they look to blaming a person, when it's really a personality!!!

So much of what I've learned came straight from the Holy Spirit. The more my relationship grew with the Lord; the more he would reveal the realm of the Spirit and how things move in the Spirit!

One of the first things the Lord said to me was, "Pay attention to detail." He told me to close my eyes and notice when light passes in front of me, to listen in stillness, to feel the breeze, to open my eyes, and unexpectedly I would see portals or vortexes! To pay attention to smells and hear his voice in thunder and the variations of lightning (fire from Heaven), the fog, his clouds on earth, the air we breathe, his breath that sustains us. How he is multifaceted, complex, complicated and simple all at the same time! The word speaks of his presence all around us.

Job 37; 2-7 says; *"**Hear attentively the noise of his voice, and the sound that goeth out of his mouth, He directeth it under the whole heaven, and his lightning unto the ends of the earth. After it a voice roareth; he thundered with the voice of his Excellency; and he will not stay them when his voice is heard. God thundered with his voice; great things doeth he which we cannot comprehend. For he saith to the***

Snow; be thou in the earth; likewise, to the small rain, and to the great rain of his strength. He sealeth up the hand of every man; that all men may know his works."

He wants us to know his very presence is all around us, his handiwork no man can emulate. He's matchless, and he is the one true God!

The Lord showed me how his people will go to counselors or take medication for a spiritual problem with a demonic root that needs to be cast out. The enemy loves the misdiagnoses of the saints! He mocks the believer and hides. He is stealthy, often going undetected! He may be living in your house, playing in your soul and your flesh! Then he waits, only to resurface to kill, steal and destroy all that he can of you!

Let's observe what our Lord Jesus discloses to us:

"Hereafter I will not talk much with you; for the

prince of this world cometh, and hath nothing in me (he has no hold over me). But that the world may know that I love the Father; and as the father gave me commandment, even so I do. Arise let us go hence (John 14:30-31).

I love this because Jesus makes it clear that the Devil has nothing in him he can use. He takes his commands from the Father, then tells his disciples, now "let's go"!

This implies that Satan can have a hold on others if he finds something in them he might use for his benefit. Here are three examples.

Acts 5: 3- "But Peter said, "Ananias, why hath Satan filled thine heart to lie to the Holy Ghost?"

Luke 22: 3- "Then Satan entered Judas called Iscariot."

Matthew 16:23- "but he turned and said unto Peter, "Get thee behind me, Satan: thou art an offense unto me."

And lastly.

1John 3:8- whoever makes a practice of sinning is of the devil.

This is a believer that practices the belief that grace is a pass to continue in sin. Things they tend to say are, "God will forgive me," and "He knows my heart."

They will use God's forgiveness to fortify their position!

If Satan has a hold in any part of our lives, he can use us! Most of the time we are unaware this is even possible!

In war some stratagems can be lethal!

For instance, as leaders and pastors, on so many

occasions, we are counseling individuals who have allowed the enemy access, and you could very well be counseling demons!! They will block a believer from receiving counsel. Satan has found something in them he can use to hinder their progress. They won't forgive others, or secret sins have left a door open for the enemy's entry!

"For we wrestle not against flesh and blood, but against principalities, against powers (forces), against the rulers of darkness of this World, against spiritual wickedness in high places (spiritual realms)" (Ephesians 6:12).

Counseling Christians with some of the same habitual problems, which roots are truly demonic! Using natural tactics to address spiritual problems. You cannot put a Band-Aid on a broken bone! The broken bone is internal; the Band-Aid only touches the surface!

For so many of us, the enemy blinds our eyes, so that even the truth contained in this scripture is hid from us. We continue to fight against people (flesh and blood), not realizing the "Prince of this World," darkens our understanding to a point where we keep aiming the finger at one another, instead of the demonic influence operating behind the scenes!

The Lord will use the natural things of this world to help direct us to things in the Supernatural. You can mentally see the Band-Aid and the broken bone!

The Gospel (the good news) teaches us that Jesus is the light of the world! This tells us that he does what you see light do in the natural. He exposes things that are hidden! The light of Christ shines within, revealing those things that are hidden in a room and in our heart. But why is it so hard for some to see?

The eye is the lamp of the body. If your vision is clear, your whole body will be full of light. But if your vision is poor, your whole body will be full of darkness. If then the light within you is darkness, how great is that darkness (Matthew 6:22-23)!

The eye is the lamp of the body. When you turn a lamp on you can see what's in the room.

When you open your eyes, you turn on the lamp, where others can see you.

The average person can look into one's eyes and see sadness, fear, lust, jealousy, pain, anger, rage, just by looking into the eyes! This is where the phrase comes from "the eyes are the windows to the soul"! Your eyes represent vision. When your vision is bad, you can't even see things that are right in front of you!

In the Spirit realm, demons are aware that your vision is off, because they know you don't see them. They mock believers and demonstrate their presence in plain view, as an insignia of their defiance against the Lord!

I remember once, after a church service, I was greeting the congregation. A very sweet older lady was in the crowd and steering in another direction away from me.

The Holy Spirit prompted me to look in her direction, go to her and greet her. I asked the people to excuse me, ran over to her, took her hand, and asked her, "How are you today?"

As I took her hand, she fell to the floor. I commanded the evil spirit (by the Holy Spirit), to leave her and it did! As this evil spirit was leaving, I felt its strong manifestation of confusion come forward, then leave!

This very sweet Lady told me that after service she was coming over to greet me, but she heard voices in her head tell her to go the other direction. The comment the demon made was, "Did she see us?"

These were demonic spirits within her conversing with one another, hoping not to be detected by the Holy Spirit (in me)!

My point in this situation is, first: her desire was to come over and greet me. The demons on the inside of her were moving her away from what they were seeing (the Holy Spirit)! Second, the Holy Spirit was pointing them out to me and leading me to go and address these demons, which I could not see with my natural eye. This led to her deliverance from this evil, controlling spirit!

All of this was taking place in the natural world that we live in, right in front of everyone, unaware! But, because of the light of Christ (formed in us), the direction of the Holy Spirit, with his prompting and his leading and the Love of God the Father, the enemy was exposed, and this beautiful lady was set free!

The Lord gets all the glory. Without him, we are left to our bondage. Whom the son sets free is free indeed! Remember, when Jesus would walk pass someone demon- oppressed, his authority forced them to manifest! To the demons it was like an explosion was passing by. They were compelled to acknowledge Jesus the Christ, the light of the world!

In war, the light exposes the darkness!!!

7

The Sound of Silence

My prayer, with the reading of this book is that one's understanding would be enlightened concerning spiritual things.

For instance, sound is so important spiritually. The definition of sound means, vibrations that travel through the air. The Greek word for air is, Pneuma, meaning spirit as well. Let's look at scripture for a minute.

"And they heard the voice (breathe, to call aloud or sound) of the LORD God walking (coming forward continually) in the garden in the cool (to smell, the wind blowing) of the day: and Adam and his wife hid themselves from the presence of the LORD God amongst the trees of the garden" (Genesis 3:8).

This scripture is saying so much about the Lord! For instance, his "Voice" was his presence, which came to Adam and Eve in the garden. God is a Spirit (air, breath) and his walking in the garden was like a loud sound of wind blowing! That was the sound of him coming. That's why they hid and were afraid!

When the Holy Spirit fell on the day of Pentecost, there was a sound of a mighty rushing wind! When the Lord showed up to Job, he was the wind in the whirlwind (a tornado); again, there was sound of a wind in the whirlwind

(Job 38; 1).

So, again, Sound is vibrations traveling in the air, as well as vibrations traveling in the spirit, or the Spirit realm!

I used to ask the Lord, "Will you teach me the things you want me to know by your Holy Spirit, concerning the spirit realm?"

With the Holy Spirit, the manifestation of "discerning of spirits" was always present with me.

I was continuously being exposed to demonic activity. I constantly needed to know with whom I was contending. The scripture says, "Satan is the prince of the power of the air" (Ephesians 2:2), knowing this, I asked the Lord to show me how the Devil moves in this.

As I mentioned earlier, the Lord told me to pay attention to detail. What does that mean? He said to me, "Close your eyes," and I did. While closed, I could sense movement in front of me: light, darkness--through my senses, it was apparent.

But I still wasn't getting it; he wanted me to be aware of what I couldn't see. We have all heard people say, "Seeing is believing."

I say, "Some things, I cannot see, yet still I believe!!!"

One day, while sitting at my computer, I heard silence. I couldn't explain this initially, but I have understanding now. The silence caught my attention, or I should say, the Holy Spirit prompted me to listen with my spirit. The silence was deafening! The Holy Spirit instructed me to tell the evil spirit in the room to manifest in the name of Jesus. Instantly the light and computer went off, a poltergeist spirit showed up at the Lord's instruction! I commanded it to go, and it did!

We have five senses: to hear, to see, smell, taste, and touch. In the natural we are so acquainted with them, but in the spiritual realm, we are oblivious!

By the Holy Spirit, you can also hear, see, smell, taste and touch! You can hear conversation, voices, noise, chatter, wind, thunder, anything you've heard in the natural, in the Spirit realm! Things familiar as well as unknown!

You can see and taste the bitterness of a vision! You can smell the foulness of a demonic being and feel his breath against your skin!

With all that being said, you can hear the sound of silence, letting you know the presence of wickedness is in the room!

Some of you have had dreams that were so real, you could hear, smell, see and taste in your dream, not comprehending that your spiritual senses were operating in the Spirit realm!

When you're not aware of the enemy and his existence in your life, like stealth he goes unnoticed, and you remain ignorant to your current situation at all times!

My desire for you is to no longer be deceived by the decorations of this world!

Hebrews 5:14 reads; "but strong meat belongeth to them that are of full age, even those who by reason

of use have their senses exercised to discern both good and evil.

What does this scripture mean in layman terms? Let me use an example!

First, we must yield to the Holy Spirit.

If your head is pounding with pain, and you've exhausted every painkiller with no results, ask the Holy Spirit to reveal to you the source. Expect an answer from the Lord. He shows you a black cloud surrounding your head, a presence hiding in the darkness!

When you see this (in the Spirit realm) he prompts you to tell it to leave; when you do, it's instant relief!

You heard and saw in the Spirit what was actually taking place, causing this headache! You yielded to the Holy Spirit, received instruction and reaped the results!

Practice consulting the Holy Spirit by using what he's given you; over time you will discern the source.

This really makes you wonder how many headaches I could have "spoken" to!

Sometimes, the way we feel is coming from another source other than what we see around us. I have had the wind blow in my house, with no doors or windows open to flow through!

While on vacation, at a four-star hotel, my bed was shaking off the floor. It only responded to me rebuking it! Devils hang out in 4-star establishments!

I have seen full manifestations of demonic beings battling in the spirit realm in front of my windshield, while driving home one night!

So much of what we see and hear around us is originating from places unseen!

Since 2008 and before, there were constant reports of the sound of trumpets coming from the sky. Reports came from the U.S, Germany, Australia, Canada, Kiev, Russia and the Philippines, to name a few. People were calling these sounds anything from aliens to angels! NASA gave its position on this from the scientific community: "These noises or sounds are but a natural phenomenon that occur all the time coming from our Earth!

But the "Word of God" stands true!

Romans 8; 22- "for we know that the whole creation groaneth (to moan jointly) and travaileth (painful and laborious effort) in pain together until now.

The earth wants its redemption because of the corruption that consumes it and waits in anticipation for the return of the Lord Jesus!

Revelation 8: 6- and the seven angels, which had the seven trumpets, prepared themselves to sound.

This scripture is powerful.

All that follows the blowing of the trumpets in Revelation will bring calamity and destruction to the earth and the inhabitants of the earth! When the angels in the Spirit realm blow these trumpets, the sound will manifest in the natural realm of the earth! But the image shows me the blowing of the trumpet is signifying a warning, sounding the alarm for war! Even when you beep a car horn, it means, "warning, beware, take notice"!

Begin to listen to the sounds around you. The sound of silence is loud!

Blow the shofar in the time of war!

8

His Voice!

I have heard so many believers say things like, "the Lord doesn't speak as frequently as some say," where others will say they've only heard his voice once, maybe twice, while yet others are still waiting to hear what everyone is talking about!

"...And the sheep follow him: for they know his voice. And a stranger they will not follow but will flee from him:" John 10:4-5.

The Lord is speaking when, where and how he sees fit!

In 1989, my daughter, Jahnae, was three months old. I put her in a car seat to do my regular routine and pick up her father from work at 11:30 pm.

While sitting in the car in a parking lot in Los Angeles, California, I heard the voice of the Lord speak to me.

It was an audible voice.

He said, *"Stand against the wiles of the Devil" (Ephesians 6:11).*

As I sat there in my car, I looked all around me. What is going on? I tried to figure out where this was coming from. It was clear. *"**Stand against the wiles of the Devil**"!*

My life at that time was so difficult--overwhelming most of the time! I kept a smile on my face to encourage myself to press through the madness! I desperately needed the Lord to intervene.

The Lord's voice was all around me in that car!

*"**Stand against the wiles of the Devil!**"* He said this to me twice! I was stunned, afraid, dazed! What in this world? I really didn't know what to

Do or say, so I looked over at my infant daughter in her car seat and said, "Jahnae, did you hear that?" She peacefully continued sleeping. I was literally learning the voice of my father. I knew I would never forget this.

Some don't believe the Lord speaks audibly today! Understandably, many believe he's so impersonal. Surprisingly, this way of thinking is in the church also.

I didn't grow up in the church; I didn't know how any of this worked, I had no expectation of how God communicates to his children! All I knew was what happened to me on that night was real!

Let's take a look at scripture.

John 12:28 (NIV) [Jesus prayed,] "Father, glorify your name!" Then a voice came from heaven, "I have glorified it, and will glorify it again." The crowd that was there and heard it said it had thundered; others said an angel had spoken to him. Jesus said, "This voice was for your benefit, not mine."

I love this scripture. First, we understand that the

Father is speaking to his Son, Jesus. When the Lord spoke, some thought it sounded like thunder, others thought it was an angel, but Jesus clarifies and says, *"This voice was for your benefit not mine!!"*

Of course, Jesus was used to communing with the Father without saying a word, or needing the Father to speak back to him out loud. This was to encourage, allow and profit the hearer to know that he speaks, aloud!! This was for my benefit on that night and I will never forget the voice of the Lord.

In the Spirit realm, communication is from spirit to spirit! When the Lord speaks to me, the only one that hears him is me! He's a personable God!

I could be in a room full of people, but I hear his voice clearly in the spirit! When I'm speaking to our congregations, at times the Lord may give me a word of wisdom, or a prophetic word that others cannot hear, but he's speaking to my spirit! God is a Spirit, that's why we are to worship him in Spirit and in truth! His voice is distinctive! It's never afraid or unaware, trying to figure out what to say to me, or apologetic for who he is! With a still, small voice, he is loud and clear! In the middle of chaos, He is not moved or frazzled! His voice remains calm, and he calms me with his voice!

Just one word, Lord, in the Battle, and we win the War!

9

Hearing aids in War

Deliverance is war! Helping someone break free of demonic oppression, possession, whatever you may struggle with is an all-out battle!

While operating in deliverance, demons manifest various ways. Some will speak verbally out of the person they are tormenting. On other occasions, they will scream, contort, spit, vomit, urinate, defecate, tremble, squirm, slither, threaten, accuse, lie, beg, intimidate or be silent, hoping not to be detected by the believer!

The gift or manifestation of discerning of spirits (which is one of the nine gifts of the Holy Spirit (1 Cor 12), enables you to see and hear good and evil in the realm of the Spirit! The Holy Spirit will let you know what demon is hiding, let you hear what the enemy is saying, at the same time showing you what's taking place at that very moment and how to strategically fight against the wiles of the enemy!!

For instance, our church has a prayer line. While we are praying for individuals, the Holy Spirit will reveal body parts to pray for, or if we command demons to come out of someone, you will see the demon (while on the prayer line) turn toward you in response to you calling his name! They hear you loud and clear!

It's as if they are inflicting pain on someone and when you identify their presence, they turn in dismay, almost as if one is startled and they'll flee!! They respond to the voice and the anointing of the believer who believes! These signs will follow them that believe (Mark 16:17).

They were caught like a thief, stealing, and you just told them to get out of that house!!

Demons can see you, but most Christians, believers, or just people in general, are so insensitive to the realm of the Spirit, these trespassers go undetected!

Your spirit man has a voice that is heard as well! So many have complained about sleeping at night and being held down, not able to physically speak or move, but once they call on the name of Jesus, in their spirit they are released!

You ask why? You just communicated with the spirit realm, without the use of your physical voice, and you were heard!! Speak boldly, out of your spirit, the enemy hears you!

Remember, we are made up of body, soul and spirit!

Your body is what we all see, and smell and touch. Your outward shell--it is your identity in the natural realm. Your skin color, your toes, hair, bad breath, hairy arms, long neck and such!

Your "soul" does most of the thinking for you, usually controlled by the body! This is where your will and emotions hide out! "I will pray today; well, maybe not." "I am just so angry I can't see straight"!

Before Christ, the flesh controlled our soul! We were just so used to doing what felt good. This is attributed to our fallen nature because of the first Adam!

Now, after Christ we are "Born Again," We start from the beginning as babies! This is why we must renew (renovate) our mind (our thoughts, feelings, and will), to become transformed into what God has purposed us to be!

Yet your spirit is where the Holy Spirit resides when we welcome the Lord Jesus into our hearts! This is why the flesh wars against the spirit. It is the old you, fighting against the Christ in you!!! Remember, we are a three part being; we are just not as familiar with our spirit man as we ought to be!

Try this exercise with me. Keep your mouth totally shut. Now ask the Lord, "Help me, Lord, to communicate more through my spirit."

Now, whom are you talking to and how? You are speaking to the Lord by your spirit! This was not coming from your imagination like a "thought," something you were seeing, an image. You are speaking spirit to spirit, from your heart, to our God!

Psalms 77; 6(b)- "I commune (meditate) with mine heart; and my spirit made diligent search."

God can speak to us right from his throne, and we can hear him!

The scripture says, "If any man has ears to hear, let him hear (Matthew 11:15)! This is not just referring to your natural ears; this means to listen carefully! It is referring to having an open spirit to receive what the Lord is really saying to us! We can't always hear with our ears, even when things are said directly to us!

While in deliverance, on many occasions, the demonic spirit will block the ears of the person being delivered, so they literally cannot hear what I am saying to them! All they can hear is that evil spirit speaking to them, telling them to leave now, to get out of there!

I first must bind the demon's influence, shut him down, and proceed with the deliverance!

He that has an ear let him hear what the Spirit of the Lord is saying!

Sometimes you're not really hearing what you think you're hearing. Someone or something else could be speaking! The enemy will infiltrate your thoughts! This is a full-time job for a demon, and they are happy to facilitate!

Relationship with the Lord will govern what you're hearing. In these cases (while in deliverance), we command the enemy to be silent and we speak the Word of God in response!

By the exercising of your senses, spending time with the Father, prayer, reading his Word--over time, the Lord's voice becomes sharper in our hearing.

The enemy makes a habit of trying to mimic or imitate the Lord, but you will know the difference, by the Holy Spirit!

Romans 8: 16- *"The Spirit himself testifies (gives evidence) with our spirit that we are God's children".*

Have you ever caught yourself tuning someone out?

They will be engaged in a conversation with you, but you've become "dull" of hearing or sluggish or lazy in your listening! A slothful spirit could be responsible! On occasion people will ask you, "Are you listening to me?" But you find yourself always drifting off or distracted by thoughts. Demons can truly be responsible!

On many occasions, when the Lord has spoken something to us, we will share it with a friend. While sharing, the enemy is listening, and your words become the plots and plans of the adversary! For example, the Lord has shown you in a vision, (in the spirit realm) you're going to receive something that you've been praying for.

When we release exclusive (God-given) things into the atmosphere (by telling someone, or broadcasting it on social media) sometimes this is the first time the enemy "caught wind of it," and he schemes to stop that word for your life, from coming to fruition!

Mark 4:15 «And these are they by the wayside, where the word is sown; but when they have heard, Satan cometh immediately, and taketh away the word (the divine expression or God's intention in this matter) that was sown in their hearts."

This scripture is a depiction of how Satan works. The Greek meaning of the word, "Word" in this text is "logos "referring to doctrine, divine expression, preaching or God's intent in a matter!

This means Satan comes after doctrine, divine expression (or revelation God gives us), preaching or God's intent!

Let me give you another example:

The Lord shows you a vision! God has voiced his conclusion in the matter! Amid your excitement, you tell someone what God has told and shown you!

Immediately Satan is out to destroy what God has

sown into your heart!! Promptly, demons are assigned to speak against the Word the Lord has given you. You constantly hear their voices destructively opposing the promise or the command!

They are seeking to wear you down to a place of unbelief! Until finally you receive the seeds, demons have spoken (believing you were talking to yourself) and you start to speak what you've heard spoken by evil spirits!

Faith comes by hearing. If you keep hearing a thing, you will believe it! It doesn't have to be true!

Decisively, you're speaking your unbelief, and finally you will have whatsoever you say!

Proverbs 18:21- "Death and life are in the power of the tongue." You will hear what you say out of your own mouth and prophesy what you hear. And this will bring life or death to your situation!

This is an everyday occurrence with most individuals by not being "watchful" to what you hear!

The enemy just deceived you into not receiving what God has ordained for you! You still don't know how it happened, and you stop trusting in the God you serve. Yet, truthfully what transpired was the adversary used your own words against you! Did you hear what I said?

Put your hearing aid on in this war!!

10

Tone-Deaf Believer

Have you ever heard of the term tone-deaf?

Sometimes, when we are speaking to someone, depending on the person or the circumstance, we will use a particular tone, based on what we are feeling or trying to convey!

When a person is "tone-deaf" or unable to distinguish differences in pitch or tone, they're not able to hear the intent of the tone, what's actually taking place!

Even if they are the one who's creating the tone! A person who sings off pitch cannot distinguish that they are "off." Yet, everyone else can!

For example, when my grandchild is running through the house, full speed, and there's a glass vase in his path of destruction, I could raise my voice in stress for fear of him breaking grandma's vase! I used the tone in my voice to control the situation! A tone is an attitude expressed by the words that someone uses in speaking or writing! Some of the synonyms for this word are quality, temper, spirit, flavor as well as mood!

A tone is important in the Spirit realm in the same

fashion it is in the natural! It displays or is symbolic of a characteristic or attitude, temperament or intent. It is distinctive!

"And even things without life-giving sound, whether pipe or harp, except they give a distinction in the sounds, how shall it be known what is piped or harped"? "For if the trumpet give an uncertain sound (tone), who shall prepare himself to the battle" (1Cor 14:7-8)?

When you hear a siren, you know an ambulance is approaching. When the fire alarm rings in school it's time to look for an exit!

I remember my grandmother saying to me as a little girl, "Watch your tone of voice!" The way I was saying "a thing" was disrespectful to her ears! It carried a tone of disrespect!

In the Spirit realm, a tone is different from sound; its pitch is distinctive!

Joshua fought the battle of Jericho. And because of the sound and the tone of the horns of the priest, and the shout of the army of the Lord's people, it spoke to the unseen forces, and the wall came tumbling down! The tone or pitch went forth in the natural, yet spoke to the supernatural, and a victory was won!

This lets you know that what we do in the physical can affect what happens in the Spirit Realm!!

When you know the authority the Father has given you over the atmosphere, over your situations, over that mountain in your life, you will address it with a certain "TONE" in your voice.

"The effectual fervent prayer of a righteous man availeth much (James 5:16)! The word, fervent means

exhibiting or marked by great intensity of feeling. The Greek word for fervent is "energeo," which means, "to be mighty in."

Your tone in this kind of prayer has sweat pouring from your brow! Remember this is the kind of prayer that will avail much!! Tones are so significant. The scripture points out more examples.

In 1Samuel 16:23- "And it came to pass, when the evil spirit from God was upon Saul, that David took a harp, and played with his hand: so, Saul was refreshed, and was well, and the evil spirit departed from him."

The tone or sound of the harp, with the anointing that was on David's life, forced the evil spirit to depart from him!

The Lord revealed to me that Satan's army responds to tones or sounds.

He showed me how "Faith" has a sound and a tone!

When you tell the enemy to get out, and he knows he must go the sound or tone of your voice, truly relying and trusting God, compels demons to get out!

Anger has a tone, rage has a tone, fear has a tone, jealousy has a tone, and the list goes on and on! With every tone or pitch, there is a reaction taking place in the spirit realm!

When chaos is all around you, and the Lord speaks in a still small voice, the tone of his voice will comfort you and reassure you that he is in control. Don't be moved by the madness, just be still, and "know that I am God!"

But it's the calmness (which has a tone) in his voice! Some of you understand what I'm saying.

The Lord wants us to be tuned into the tone (the

level of intensity) in the realm of the spirit!

When he's calling your name, you can't continue to be tone-deaf, or you will miss the sound of his call!

For example;

I Samuel 3:8,[A] *third time the Lord called, "Samuel!" And Samuel got up and went to Eli and said, "Here I am; you called me. Then Eli realized that the Lord was calling the boy. So Eli told Samuel, "Go and lie down, and if he calls you, say, 'Speak, Lord, for your servant is listening.*

"Speak Lord, for your servant is listening!" When the commander in chief, the Lord of the army says to you softly, "Run," the tone tells you to move quietly.

In this war, tone is everything, they must not see you coming, and if they see you coming and you say MOVE, by your tone they must "get thee behind you"!!!

11

Warring in my sleep!

In the natural realm, there are various ways in which we communicate through our physical body: a smile, a winking of the eye, a waving of the hand and speech are just a few.

In the spirit realm it's from one spirit to another, or from your spirit into the spirit realm!! The body is not relevant like it is in the natural! Let us look at scripture.

In 2 Corinthians 12:2 the Apostle Paul says, *"I know a man in Christ who fourteen years ago, whether in the body I do not know, or out of the body I do not know, God knows, such a man was caught up to the third heaven. And I know how such a man, whether in the body or apart from the body I do not know, God knows, was caught up into Paradise and heard inexpressible words, which a man is not permitted to speak."*

The man he was alluding to was himself. The encounter was "in the Spirit," hence the meaning, ' caught up!' This was taking place in Heaven, where the Lord is, and whether his body was there or not, he was not aware; his words were; *"I cannot tell; only God knows."*

In this place, He would see visions and revelations! He was moving by his spirit in the Spirit realm, not limited by his body, but able to be in Heaven seeing visions and receiving revelations!

I love this for so many reasons! I have such a respect and regard for the Apostles, prophets and disciples of old!

They truly were the pillars of the Gospel. Jesus Christ was the cornerstone, the blueprint, he laid his life, (this body) down, and the disciples followed his lead! And we have reaped where we have not sown! Thank you, Lord!

The Bible gives us a glimpse of what's really going on around us all the time. The Lord is always showing his people how he communicates!

He still speaks to us through visions and revelations.

A vision is an experience of seeing someone or something in a dream or trance, or as a supernatural spirit being!

A revelation is the divine or supernatural disclosure to humans of something relating to human existence or the world. It is a surprising and previously unknown fact.

Again, He speaks to us from his Spirit to our spirit!

I constantly ask the Lord questions, bombarding heaven with every thought! One of these questions was:

"When we go to sleep at night, why does the enemy attack so many in their dreams"?

Well, let's look at what happens when we sleep.

According to scientists who study chemicals and body functions of a human being, when we sleep there are a series of events that take place in the brain.

First there are two stages of sleep, slow wave sleep (SWS) known as deep sleep, and Rapid Eye Movement, (REM), known as dreaming sleep.

When we first lie down, close our eyes, our muscles become relaxed and we eventually go into a deep sleep! Our heart rate is slower and our breathing is slow and deep. This eventually triggers our brain into a state of unconsciousness, which leads us into this dreaming sleep!

The Word says, "Jesus Christ is the same yesterday, today and forever" (Hebrews 13:8).

The word "same" means to breathe unconsciously and constantly. Jesus is consistent, like breathing when you sleep, like your air that sustains you!!

When "REM" or dreaming sleep takes place, scientists say they are baffled and curious! One's breathing and heart rate becomes erratic, and the muscles become paralyzed, while the brain becomes highly active!!

This is an area experts are still trying to figure out. Remember, mankind is only discovering what God has already done!

So many people are puzzled about what happens in their dreams! They are experiencing smells, and fighting, and running and strange sensations!!

How is it possible, if in this state of dreaming, while your physical muscles are paralyzed, are you running, talking, fighting and falling? Maybe the mind plays tricks on us? I think not!

When you close your eyes at night, you are still able to see images! When we are in this state of sleep, the enemy tries to infiltrate, because our defenses are down! But your spirit man is capable and willing, and he doesn't need your physical body to maneuver! The Spirit is willing; it's the flesh that's weak!

Let me take a detour;

In 2 Corinthians 10:5, I find one of the most informative scriptures for a believer.

The scripture says: **"Casting *down (destroying) imaginations, and every high thing that exalteth itself against the knowledge (knowing God) of God and bringing into captivity every thought to the obedience of Christ (2 Corinthians 10:5).***

The word imaginations in this text means to compute or reason thoughts consciously!

Okay, so let me be more precise.

The word is telling us, when you have a thought or imagination about a person, place or thing, and it's speaking to you something that does not line up with the Word of God, knowing God,(based on his word) then you are to make that thought (take it captive) comply with the Word of God! The enemy is speaking to you! Come against it!!

An example:

You are driving your car; you have a thought, telling you to drive off the bridge! The scripture says, *"My times (duration, beginning and end) are in thy hand" (Psalms 31:15)*! To drive off a bridge would be murder, self-murder! We know the Lord does not agree with murder. This is the enemy speaking, taunting you, the same way he did our Lord Jesus in the wilderness! What would Jesus do?

The question is what did Jesus do?

Matthew 4:1-4 "

Then Jesus was led by the Spirit into the wilderness to be tempted [a] by the devil. ² After fasting forty days and forty nights, he was hungry. ³ The tempter came to him and said, "If you are the Son of God, tell these stones to become bread."

⁴ Jesus answered, "It is written: 'Man shall not live on bread alone, but on every word that comes from the mouth of God.'"

He spoke back to the "fowler" (Psalm 91:3) and recited the "Word" to the Devil! When the Lord would say, "it is written', he was saying to the enemy, (and referring to the Old Testament) that God has already addressed your lies and deception in this matter!

He spoke back to the enemy!

This is one of the things we don't bother to do!

We will hear a thought come into our mind, and we will either ignore it or receive it and speak life to it!

If you hear a voice in your head tell you that you're going to die tonight, you don't just receive what you hear and act on it without knowing the source or the voice! "Well, I better get my house in order, let me say my goodbyes"! No, you will not! You will rebuke that voice, in the name of Jesus and forbid it to speak any longer!

Remember, this is war!!! You are in the trenches and don't even know it!!

Satan will give you a thought, waiting for you to speak it and agree with him (Amos 3:3)! Oh, he desperately just wants you to agree!! This is the snare of the fowler!

Satan, your adversary, knows the Word too!

This is one of his oldest ploys in the book! He will twist or pervert the word. Every word that proceeds out of the mouth of God!!

He did it to Eve in the Garden, and he tried it with Jesus in the wilderness. This makes you and me candidates as well!

We are not ignorant of his devices; we just don't comprehend he's using them on us!! Some of these crazy conversations (you are having with yourself) are coming from a demonic source!

You can have a fleeting thought that you initiate on your own, but when it's the enemy operating, he will continue to pursue you, until you either yield to his thought or confront him with the Word!

Submit to God, resist (oppose, to stand against) the devil, and he will flee (vanish, run away) from you (James 4:7)!!

Ok now, let's go back to sleep!

As I stated previously, the enemy works in our thoughts and imaginations, when we're asleep, and in a deep sleep is an opportune time for his imps, demons, evil spirits to work on your thoughts and imagination! This is one reason why we should pray before we go to sleep, that we might dwell in peace and safety in the Lord! This 18th century prayer was created for children and has been handed down through the years:

"Now I lay me down to sleep, I pray the Lord my soul to keep, if I should die before I wake, I pray the Lord my soul to take" amen.

Someone had the right idea and was mindful of our providence or frailty when we sleep!

Your body may be subdued, but your spirit is alive and well, contending on your behalf! You are fighting the good fight in your dreams! This is why it's important to sow to the spirit, and build up your inner man (that's been born again) exceedingly!

As a pastor, whenever I have a parent or a child come to me with problems in their sleep, nightmares, night terrors on various occasions, I have them speak scripture before they go to sleep!

"I will both lay me down in peace, and sleep: for thou Lord, only makest me dwell in safety (Psalms 4:8).

The "Word of God' is an antidote for what ails us! It is your weapon in this **war**! In other cases, we would command evil spirits to vacate the premises or the person. Whatever weapon is needed, the Holy Spirit would direct us and provide the treatment! The one thing that is mandatory after we submit to God is to oppose or stand against the enemy! Do not act as if he's not harassing you. If you ignore him, he will **not go away**! I repeat, he will **not go away**!! He hasn't because you won't shut him down! Resist him with your "sword"! Forbid him! Rebuke him; silence him, in the name of Jesus!!

If the Lord tells us to bring him in remembrance of his own word (Isaiah 43:26), then you must know he expects you to remind the Devil of God's "Word" also!!

When you are asleep and the enemy is attacking, know this: Jesus (the Word, who is seated in heavenly places) is ever interceding for you! While at the same time, the Holy Spirit, (who is the restrainer, helper, very breath of God) which lives in your spirit, is alive and well. He will fight for you in your dreams! So rest in him with sweet peace in Jesus!!

This is just a reminder that the **war** continues, even while you sleep.

Sticks and stones may not break the enemy's bones, but the Word will annihilate him!!!

The Lord is warring even in your sleep!

12

The Works of the flesh

Demons and evil spirits are responsible for a lot that goes on in this world! Their influence and presence is undeniable, yet so many are ignorant of the Devils devices! They are loveless creatures, which thrive on the ignorance of the believer! We are the light of this world, as believers. If we can't see, how can we help our brother out of this darkness?

With the presence of demons and evil spirits as an influence in many situations, the church has got to be aware, informed, equipped to address the obvious. The truth is, in the local church, deliverance, (CASTING OUT DEMONS) is taboo! I really have a problem when I see a spirit in action in the pulpit! Speaking over God's people, dropping seeds of error! Seeds that produce an infected harvest! Words are seeds and in the realm of the spirit they will reproduce after their own kind.

For one, the Lord will expose who's really speaking

to his people, so you will not believe every voice that you hear, and secondly it will help you access or address the real culprit!

For many in the "Body of Christ," demons or evil spirits are never considered as being the problem! The reason for this social exclusion is, if they are the problem, what is the solution? Because we are not sure how to deal with or resolve this issue concerning demonic influence, people are left in bondage!

There have been countless times in which I have witnessed a religious spirit operating in the church!

I am still perplexed to hear believers say a Christian cannot have a demon! I have heard so many excuses or theories as to why one cannot have evil spirits residing with them, yet they will walk out the church doors and go home and struggle with pornography for twenty years! Others would say, 'Well, that's the works of the flesh, spoken about in the book of Galatians 5:19!'

" Now the works of the flesh are manifest, which are these: Adultery, fornication, uncleanness, lasciviousness, idolatry, witchcraft, hatred, variance, emulations, wrath, strife, seditions, heresies, envyings, murders, drunkenness, revellings, and such like:, of the which I tell you before, as I have also told you in time past, that they which do such things shall not inherit the kingdom of God.

The Lord spoke a word to me on the "works of the flesh." The more we participate in the works of the flesh, by yielding our members, that spirit behind it will become our master! After a while, your master takes you captive at his will (2 Tim 2: 26)! He told me at this point the characteristics (features or qualities that identify a person, place or thing) are demons or demonic. For over 30 years I have dealt with the enemy in the field of deliverance and I understand why some leaders in the church struggle. When you have a congregation, they expect you to have all the answers to life itself, and, of course, that is not the case, but pride will not allow them to seek the Lord past their own theology! They do not operate in "casting out demons" and they rationalize the process. In this lies the process; let's look at the Truth, the Word of God.

The people approached Jesus as he was casting out a devil, and they were accusing him of casting out devils by a demon, Jesus responded:

Luke 11; 17- But he, knowing their thoughts, said unto them, every kingdom divided against itself is brought to desolation; and a house divided against a house falleth. If Satan also divided against himself, how shall his kingdom stand? Because ye say that I cast out devils through Beelzebub (a name of Satan). And if I by Beelzebub cast out devils, by whom do your sons cast them out? Therefore, shall they be your judges. But if I with the finger of God cast out devils, no doubt the Kingdom of God is come upon you.

First the Lord is pointing out that devils come from Satan's kingdom! Satan is trying to advance his kingdom! Surely, he's not going to run his workers out of a building, or a house (your temple) when he has them doing the construction! Or better said, the destruction! The best part of the process in casting out demons is the "FINGER OF GOD"! When he touches, the kingdom is upon you! The Kingdom of God just smacked the Kingdom of Darkness, and Satan's workers had to flee!

But how does this apply to a Christian, if he can't have a demon? We say things like, "this is the temple of the Holy Ghost (1Cor 6: 19), "light and darkness cannot dwell in the same place." This kind of teaching of the scripture stops one from getting deliverance and affords the enemy the opportunity to become a stronghold (mindset) that keeps many in oppression!

Look at 1 Corinthians 6: 15, - "*Know ye not that your bodies are the members (a part) of Christ? Shall I then take the members of Christ, and make them the members of a harlot? God forbids. What? Know ye not that he, which is joined to a harlot, is one body? For two, saith he, shall be one flesh. But he that is joined unto the Lord is one spirit!! Flee fornication. Every sin that a man doeth is without the body; but he that committeth fornication sinneth against his own body.*

Again, whom you yield your members to becomes your master! When you yield your body to a harlot, that demonic spirit behind the harlotry becomes your master. You are now one flesh, one body! Your spirit as a believer is one with the Lord, but you just joined your body with the demonic. Light and darkness are dwelling in two separate places. **But all of it is you**!

1Corinthians 6:20- *"For you are bought with a price: therefore, Glorify God in your body and in your spirit, which are God's.*

You see, if you're a Christian, all of you belong to

God by right, but it's up to you what you do with all of you! He tells you to glorify him, but many choose not to!

More scripture:

1John 3:7-8- "Little children, let no man deceive you; he that doeth righteousness is righteous, even as he is righteous. He that committeth (practice) sin is of the devil; for the devil sinneth from the beginning. For this purpose, the Son of God was manifested, that he might destroy the works of the devil.

No one can continue to practice sin and not be snared by the devil.

As a believer we must walk in the power of the Holy Spirit and contend with these evil forces! The Lord has given us the weapons, "Put on the whole armor," Ephesians 6, and contend, fight back! If not now, then when; the time is now!

When the Lord returns, there will be no need for deliverance (casting out devils) driving them out of our lives, trespassers that deceive even the most brilliant of men!

One day this War will come to an end!
And we win!

13

Turn it off!!

Now this is one of my favorite things to do. On a cool October evening, get some hot cocoa, cuddle with my husband, and watch a great movie. This is what I call unwinding in front of the TV.

On the TV you can watch anything from warm stories of inspiration, to violent sexually explicit material that makes your heart shudder!

I can imagine in biblical days, they watched the sky and the moon and the stars; that was their TV screen, and they entertained themselves. Today all facets of madness and suggestive thoughts that are brought to you by this box stimulate your imagination!

Don't get me wrong, there are some shows that preach the Word and teach the Word and encourage us in some of our darkest hours, giving you what you need to lift your spirit! It is just a channel away!

Yet, the devil will always pervert (twist) anything he can use!

I remember when I got filled with the Holy Spirit; I was attending a COGIC church in California. What a glorious day that was for me! There was a lot of tradition in the church and I didn't know the difference between what God was saying and what man implemented.

The rules they had were so eccentric! I was a baby Christian, so whatever they said, I did. I followed the rules. You couldn't wear pants, and no makeup, don't show your toes, or too much skin. It can cause a man of God to fall! Women could only be missionaries and last but not least, you couldn't go to the movies!!

The movies! Now that was just ridiculous to me! I was young in the Lord and in my twenties.

I loved going to the movies or watching them from home. As I grew in my walk with the Lord, I realized how my eyes were "wide shut"!

We live in a world full of distractions!

In the word, **Mark 8:36, says, *"For what shall it profit a man, if he shall gain the whole world, and lose his own soul?***

The Greek word for world is "Kosmos." One of the meanings of this word is decoration or adorning, implying the world is one big adorned, decorated mass!!

When something is decorated, it's covering up what's hidden. The Lord told me we like to be entertained, by this decorated, concealed world, and it is our diversion! It turns us away from our intended course!

Because the enemy, the adversary, the Devil is a deceiver, distraction is his middle name! We are so busy looking at how pleasing the fruit looks to our eyes; it's adorned in a way that prevents us from seeing what is veiled!

Henceforth, what we call TV, or television is defined as, a system for transmitting visual images and sound that are reproduced on screens, chiefly used to broadcast programs for entertainment, information, and education.

The messages are so subtle; on TV you're hardly aware of what's taking place. For instance, **Matthew 5:27-28 reads** – *"Ye have heard that is was said by them of old time, thou shalt not commit adultery: But I say unto you, that whosoever looketh on a woman to lust after her hath committed adultery with her already in his heart."*

In Job 31:1, Job said, *"I made a covenant (to clearly render) with mine eyes; why then should I think upon a maid?"*

The Lord told me, when a man looks on a woman and lusts after her, by entertaining pornography or other avenues, he makes a covenant, he signs a contract with his eyes!

Pornography biblically means "the writings of a harlot"! Watching pornography is making a covenant with your eyes with a harlot! It's also committing adultery just by the act of "looking" on one and lusting in your heart!

This covenant that is formed is an agreement! How can two walk unless they agree? (Amos 3:3) The two that are agreeing is the one looking and the demon spirit that is dangling the carrot! These demons will visit you by flooding your soul with images and pictures, progressing into acts of masturbation with these images and pictures, until sin is conceived where you are partaking of the forbidden fruit! This is just one aspect of how the demonic realm operates!

This spirit produces soul ties in the realm of the spirit! Your soul is intertwined with the adulterous image, which takes the place of a wife or husband! This spirit will have you spending time away with yourself and all the fantasies this demon desires for you. Take heed with an open heart!

This is why you don't necessarily need a physical body to cheat on your spouse; you have a demonic one that no one can see, not even

You! You have a soul tie in the realm of the spirit with a demonic spirit that pleasures you! This is why it's hard to break in the natural, because the contract is demonic...you can only suppress it in the natural, but spiritual weapons can destroy this demon!!

Being single does not exempt you either. I have witnessed this on many occasions, where women will come to me with an ongoing experience of knowing they are having physical intimacy on a regular basis with a spirit being! I just call it devils! Incubus is its name! They made a movie about him in 2016!

The counterpart for men will show up in what many have called "wet dreams" this spirit is called Succubus!

These are manifestations of what's taking place in the spirit realm, touching the natural realm! I know, this may be a lot to absorb, but this is simply one of the ways we allow demonic oppression!

This is war!

This is a standard tactic of the enemy! As long as he can keep us in a place of shame about these kinds of things that plague us, we will remain in bondage or a slave to our private sins.

This scenario goes from looking to yearning to undertaking!

James 1:14-15 says – *"But every man is tempted when he is drawn away of his own lust and enticed. Then when lust have conceived (to catch or to seize you), it bringeth forth sin; and sin, when it is finished bringeth forth death!* In the spirit realm, the enemy walked right into your marriage, subtly, using a Victoria Secret model on your TV set!

Yet, Job was guarding his heart, by guarding his eyes (Job 31:1)! He wasn't filled with the "Holy Spirit" like we are today who will " check us on a dime" or tell us to "stop looking"! But even if we miss the mark and fall, we can still get free of the clutches of the enemy in this WAR!!

A lot of times, while calling demons out in a deliverance session, when you command adultery to come out you can call pornography out as well!

The Devil and his demons thrive, animate and exist in your TV!

They entertain us and transmit visual images and sounds to subdue you and ultimately reside in your domain! The sins that are practiced: fornication, murder, hatred, to name a few on your TV, make you numb to its spiritual outcome for your soul (your mind, will and emotions)!

We are submitting to a demonic spirit entertaining us with sin. Now, that's the truth. The Holy Spirit will set us free if we let him!

Some of you have noticed when you fell asleep with the TV left on and woke up to realize you were dreaming about the horror show that was on your set! This is not a happenstance; this is a transmission on the spiritual airways!!

The Lord told me that in these last days, demons were going to announce themselves in plain sight. Just look at some of the titles of shows listed for your viewing pleasure. It's not hidden.

Job was guarding his heart by guarding his eyes, what about you?

Turn the channel or turn it off!

This is one of Satan's weapons of war!

14

Portals

A **portal is** an entrance and opening, a gateway from one realm to another. We have highways and inter-states, planes, trains and automobiles as means of travel here in this earth, but my focus in this book is coming from a spiritual perspective. In Genesis 28:12 Jacob had a dream about God's angels. *"**And he dreamed, and behold a ladder (staircase) set up on the earth, and the top of it reached to Heaven; and behold the angels of God ascending and descending on it.***"

Another scripture that shows the angels in motion, John 1:51- *"**And he said unto you, Hereafter ye shall see heaven open and the**

Angels of God ascending and descending upon the son of man."

The Holy Spirit would remind me of things I may have forgotten about the angels by the Word of God. The angels going back and forth, how they would bring a word to God's people to encourage, or direct, or to instruct. How they showed up at the tomb of Jesus and rolled away the stone (in the natural)! How they strengthened Jesus in the Garden of Gethsemane (Matthew 4:11), and the list continues!

I have been walking with the Lord for 35 years now, and I am constantly learning about the vastness of the spirit realm! The Lord revealed to me that a portal has force behind it! Like a wind of air, a vortex, air moving in a direction. Demons are spirits, (from the Greek word Pneuma) meaning air. These evil spirits are in motion and travel from one realm to the other. The portal is a doorway.

These portals would appear to me, wherever and whenever! The Holy Spirit would reveal them to me! At first, I wondered why I continued to see openings, or doorways in front of me! The portals could be different sizes and shapes. Whenever I would see one, the Lord would direct me to command it to be closed and cover the entrance with the blood of Jesus! His blood is alive!

He would teach me things I did not always understand, but I would obey! I knew I had a lesson to be learned in it.

By the Holy Spirit, he would show me a box in the Spirit realm. I believe I would see these boxes for years and not know what I was looking at! The more I would grow in the things of the Lord, by reading his word, praying in the spirit (in tongues) and in the natural, fasting, I realized nothing was normal in my life anymore!

I would see the trees bending and praising the Lord; he would show me in the spirit!

Scripture tells you so many secrets in the word, but revelation exposes truths!

"**And *he answered and said unto them, I tell you***

that, if these should hold their peace, the stones would immediately cry out" (Luke 19:40).

I would hear what the birds were singing by his Holy Spirit, and the Lord would show me these portals where demons would pass through to this dimension, inflicting their havoc on God's creation!

It is a whole other world, but it's spiritual! And our God is the father of Spirits!

A portal is a gateway! Witches today and the occult seek them out on a regular basis. They channel in demons to assist them in their sorceries and divination, astral projection, tarot cards to Ouija boards, horoscopes to spiritual guides--they are all rooted in the demonic, and demonic forces are the source of them all!

Regardless of the weapon, we still have authority to shut the enemy down in his tracks!!

Saturate your home with prayer and always seek the Lord for every strategy in every situation! Remember, the Holy Spirit has an arsenal for whatever the enemy is coming with!

While portals can be used by the enemy as gateways to the lost sheep, Christ is the door to salvation, a Shepherd to his sheep. Make sure the sheep gate is closed; as Jesus leads, be sure to follow!

Remember, this is war!!!

15

We will know, as
we are known!

When I was in my forties, I had to move to the country, rural Virginia, with my three kids for two years.

The country was peaceful to me; it was a sense of comfort for me, but it was far from civilian life. The nearest store was 20 miles.

I had to drive five hours a day back and forth to work five days a week, while I pastored a small church an hour away on weekends! I was fatigued to say the least.

During this drive time, I spent hours talking and communing with the Holy Spirit!

He truly is my friend, and my saving grace!

One of the gifts of the Holy Spirit is discerning of spirits. This gift allows you to see and hear good and evil, demons and angels, places, and things! This is a supernatural perception in the spirit realm or the realm of spirits!

One night while driving home, I saw a demonic

spirit pass in front of the car, as if he was walking out of the spirit realm, into our atmosphere, then back into the Spirit realm. It was as if he was just passing through. I began to pray in tongues, as I continued to drive.

I started to notice a car behind me.

Now driving in the country at night, it is pitch black! These lights on the car behind me kept getting my attention. I'm looking through the rear-view mirror, the lights were getting closer and closer, until finally the lights were so close, I could see there was no car attached to the lights!! This was crazy! Two lights directly behind my car, so close they could hit my car!! I commanded the evil spirits to go in the name of Jesus, and instantly they left! That's what I call a crazy ride home!!

Discerning of spirits allowed me to see and experience this in the natural realm.

Demons are aware of you, but we are insensitive to their existence!

All of us human beings, mankind, have experienced difficult situations in our lives at one time or another. Aunt Pearl used to say, "If you haven't, (been through something difficult) keep on living, you will!"

There was a time in my life when I went through an unexpected divorce after 23 years of marriage. I became a single parent, who was a believer in Jesus Christ, and was overwhelmed with life's difficulties, but determined to be an example, provider, and an overcomer for my children's sake!

Because of my relocating, and my commute to work each day, I would leave at 4:00 am and return home at 11:30 pm each night!

My youngest daughter, Hope, (who was seven years old at the time) and I, shared an upstairs loft bedroom. I had a 23-year-old, (Brittney) and a 19-year-old daughter (Jahnae) in college, and a 17-year-old son (Christen) completing high school! Pressure from every direction, and the Lord had instructed me to open my first school of the prophets'!

On the weekends I would run, "The School of the Prophets," help my daughter with homework, cook dinner, love on my kids, pass out, and start all over again on Monday! My mind and physical body were spent!

This was my state or condition.

One night I got home a little early and was determined I would get some real sleep! The loft bedroom overlooked the dining room beneath us, so I could see and hear all movement in the house at any given time!

This particular night, at 3:00 am I awoke from my sleep to the sound of a large crash!! It literally sounded like an airplane had hit the house!

I jumped up out of my bed and ran to the window, to see what happened! There was nothing there! I looked over the balcony of the loft, not a thing was moving!

My daughter was asleep, not stirred by this crashing sound! The house was quiet; I could not believe that no one heard this crash but me!!!!

Not knowing what else to do, I went back to bed. As soon as I lay down, I heard this demonic voice; it called me a name, it cursed at me, calling me a female dog! I instantly felt myself jump up!

The amazing thing about this was, when I jumped up I instantly knew what to do, I found myself against the wall in the room, at the top of the wall, almost touching the ceiling, ready to fight! I looked on the bed and my body was there asleep, my daughter was there asleep in her bed as well, but I only focused on encountering the demon in the room! Literally it was like a matrix moment! I know for some who haven't dealt in the spirit realm this sounds crazy, not natural, but its supernatural and it's real!

I commanded this spirit, in the Name of JESUS, to go, and he screamed and cursed as he faded out, literally!! I heard his voice and saw his black image be sucked back into a vortex, like a vacuum or tunnel, until he dissolved into silence! It looked like a scene from a movie!

This evil spirit was sent for this encounter, and I was so aware of the realm he operated in! It was concerning to me. How did I know exactly how to respond?

I struggled with how I knew what to do; it was like I was in my element.

I later realized that our "spirit man" is capable and designed for things of the spirit-realm! We are "body, soul and spirit." The spirit side of you is where the Holy Spirit resides! This opens you up to fight, war, and move, to know and be known in the realm of the spirit!

Broken, bruised, exhausted warriors are in this war! And we still fight!

16

There is life, after life!

As a pastor, I have officiated too many funerals. I truly prefer weddings; this focuses on a union, while funerals point towards a separation.

However, in the scripture, ***Ecclesiastes 7:4, reads, "The heart of the wise is in the house of mourning."***

There is so much truth in this statement! I've noticed that sometimes, the only time that some families come together is if someone passes away. We will unite and reflect on the life of our loved one. We seek forgiveness with a distant cousin or promise to make an effort to be more "in touch." We acknowledge our frailty as humans; the reality sinks in: this time here on earth is not forever! The heart becomes wise in the house of mourning.

While writing this portion of the book, the Lord spoke to me about "passing away."

Why do we even use the term passing away instead of die, or died, more often?

So many have a view in their mind's eye of what we will experience, what will happen to our physical body, how and where we will exist, or if we will exist at all?

The words die, or died, or dead for some is just too harsh to hear! If someone passed away, they must have passed from one place to the other!

It helps the hearer, but I referenced the scripture for comfort sake!

To pass away goes back as far as 1375 in the old English way of speaking, meaning one has departed!

John 11:25-26, "Jesus said, I am the resurrection and life, He that believes in me, though he were dead, yet shall he live!"

One of the Greek words used here for 'dead' in this text is 'Apo'! It's definition means "here after" or away from a place or time or relation; it also means a reversal.

This would make the scripture read like so;

John 11; 25- "He that believes in me, though he were (away from (this) place, time and relations", yet shall he live!

The loved one may not be here anymore, but they live somewhere else! Meaning separated from earth, over here, but living on somewhere else!

This place is in the realm of the spirit.

Again, another biblical definition for the Greek word 'Apo' or

'Dead', is the word reversal! Meaning a reversal of the journey of life!

This lines up with the scripture that says, *"Before I formed thee in the belly, I knew thee" (Jeremiah 1:5)!*

Furthermore:

"You watched me as I was being formed in utter

seclusion, as I was woven together in the dark of the womb" (Psalm 139:15).

The Lord knew us, formed and fashioned us before we were a substance! Death is reversing the course. We are returning to the one who formed us! This lets us know we will continue on after death!

When God breathed into man, he became a living soul! The spirit-life that was breathed into man will go back to the Lord, this is the reversal!

The soul will reside with the Lord or (after judgment) in a lake of fire! It is based on our choosing. While the flesh will return to the dust!

In the **Book of Revelation 21:8 – it reads, "But as for the cowardly, the faithless, the detestable, as for murderers, the sexually immoral, sorcerers, idolaters, and all liars, their portion will be in the lake that burns with fire and sulfur, which is the second death.**

This would be the sum of all our choices!

But the "you" that everyone knows will live on forever, somewhere!

I say this to those who have loved ones who died in the Lord! We have hope based on the scriptures.

1 Thessalonians 4:13-18

¹³ But I would not have you to be ignorant, brethren, concerning them, which are asleep, that ye sorrow not, even as others, which have no hope.¹⁴ For if we believe that Jesus died and rose again, even so them also which sleep in Jesus will God bring with him.¹⁵ For this we say unto you by the word of the Lord, that we which are alive and remain unto the coming of the Lord shall not prevent them which are asleep.¹⁶ For the Lord himself shall descend from heaven with a shout, with the voice of the archangel, and with the trump of God: and the dead in Christ shall rise first: [17] Then we which are alive and remain shall be caught up together with them in the clouds, to meet the Lord in the air: and so shall we ever be with the Lord. Wherefore we are to comfort one another with these words.

As a believer in Jesus Christ, truly one of my favorite scriptures is Matthew chapter 28. In this chapter, Jesus has already been crucified and his body has been placed in a tomb. Mary Magdalene and Mary arrive at the tomb only to be greeted by an angel who says," *For I know that ye seek Jesus, which was crucified, He is not here; for he is risen, as he said" (Mt 28; 5)!* The word "risen" in the Greek is "egeiro." It means to rouse from sleep, from sitting, from lying, from disease, from inactivity, from nonexistence to awake from death, to stand!

When we pass from here to there, some are literally rising up from diseases that seemed to end their lives, yet they really are standing up on the other side! Death cannot hold "the believer" down, he shall Stand up; rise again, because Jesus said so!

Whew!! Now with that I am screaming Halleluiah!!!

The Angel of the Lord is reminding them He has risen, just like he said! This is paramount to us all who believe! He "has risen" JUST LIKE HE SAID! He fulfilled his promise to his disciples, and now he is the firstfruit, or the first one who has risen from the dead, letting us know we will rise too! To die, for the believer, is to rise again!

In the realm of the spirit, we are shedding these old

grave clothes, because we have to get up!!

As I was writing this, the Holy Spirit woke me up this morning to this part of the chapter, **Matthew 28:20- "I am with you always, even until the end of the world."** He wanted to remind me to tell you this!

The world "always" in this scripture comes from the Greek word "pas" which means: whenever, whatsoever, whosoever, any, daily, by all manner and means. He will be with us, when we "pass" from the natural to the spirit realm, even until the end, Jesus will be there!

We are aware that there is life after life on this earth! But if we know this, shouldn't we better prepare for what comes next?

Deuteronomy 30: 19- I call heaven and earth to record this day against you, that I have set before you life and death, blessing and cursing: therefore choose life, that both thou and thy seed may live:

After this war, in the end, you shall live again!

17

The Air Around you

The natural and the spiritual realms are so intertwined; at times it would be like separating soul from spirit!

For example:

Then the LORD God formed man of the dust from the ground and breathed (to inflate) into his nostrils the breath of life (divine inspiration, soul); and man became a living being (Genesis 2:7).

Notice God breathed into his (man's) nostrils. This is actually the natural way we breathe, through your nose, not the mouth. Through this we became intertwined.

Before we were a living soul, we were red clay! We are the breath of God mixing with red dirt! What a creator!

In Psalms 139:14 it says, "I will praise thee; for I am fearfully and wonderfully made: marvelous are thy works; and that my soul knoweth right well."

I cannot imagine the experience Adam must have encountered. He was made as a full man, not an infant. What God and Adam talked about had to be pretty interesting!

God blew air, his Spirit into the dirt (red clay) and the dirt became alive!! He uses everything around us! He made all things, and all things were made for him!

"All things were made by him; and without him was not any thing made that was made" (John 1:3).

For by him were all things created, that are in heaven, and that are in earth, visible and invisible, whether they be thrones, or dominions, or principalities, or powers: all things were created by him, and for him (Colossians 1:16):

When I started to think about the fact that the Lord breathed and it made me, and used the air, his breath, to sustain me, I wanted to know everything I could about AIR! Just the fact that we need air to even exist, amazes me!

The Holy Spirit keeps throwing scripture in my direction!

Psalms 104:29-31-

When you hide your face, they panic; when you take away their breath, they die and return to dust. When you send your Spirit, they are created, and you renew the face of the earth!

If God takes away our breath, we die and return to dust: this is the truth!

We are dust! The red clay that we are made from contains all of the minerals our body needs. Minerals come from the earth: dirt and water! Scientists use different forms of mining to extract minerals today, and package them as supplements that we might need in our daily diet, our "DIRT DIET" as well as various foods we eat!

Plants and animals supply the vitamins that we need. Vitamins and minerals are essential nutrients. Working together, they perform hundreds of functions in the body. They help support your bones and skeletal structure, heal wounds, and strengthen and restore your immune system. They help to repair cellular damage while converting food into energy!

When the Lord made us, he supported us with everything that surrounds us! God is amazing, how he takes care of his creation!

Truly, God is a wonder; he is the chief engineer of all things! I am in awe of his supreme and independent power, his sovereignty!!

Every part of your body needs oxygen to survive. It is carried throughout the body by red blood cells in your bloodstream.

Oxygen cannot get into your blood directly through the skin, so a complex technique in your lungs absorbs it from the air and transfers it into your bloodstream.

The process of taking air into the lungs is called inhalation or inspiration, and the process of breathing it out is called exhalation or expiration.

It's almost like we take in the inspiration, use what's needed, and breathe out what has expired or is of no use to us anymore.

Since this is a book about War and the spirit realm you might ask 'where is the warfare in this?' Well, let's look at one aspect.

Satan also works through the air. The air we breathe has agents working in the background. Our air is filled with contaminates! Every other week CDC (The Center for Disease Control) comes out with a new strand of this or that!

Doctors and scientists have stated over and over again the dangers of secondhand smoke! Inhaling smoke from cigarettes that circulates through the atmosphere, where a non-smoker is breathing, has proven to be life threatening! Someone else is smoking the cigarette, and others reap the malicious results of your habit! The innocent victims! Satan is a deceiver.

I used to work for the airline industry, and years ago, in the cabin of the plane they would seat non-smokers in the front, and smokers in the back of the plane. But you could still smell the smoke circulating through the cabin! There was no way around it! Finally, the industry decided there would no longer be smoking permitted on flights! If you go to a club or a bar, the smoke will stick to your clothes, your hair, everything! Anything that sticks or lingers around in the spirit realm has gotta go!

You can't just breathe any kind of air in!!

To stay alive, we must breathe! This much we know is true! Viruses and all sorts of bacteria (live organisms) can be passed through the air we breathe because "Air" is alive!! Notice, again, that things are passed through the air!

Satan is the prince (chief ruler), of the power (forces) of the air (Ephesians 2: 2). The air that's referred to in this text is the Greek word "aer." This means, the lower, denser air, indicating the location of where Satan is the chief ruler.

There are three Heavens referenced in scripture. The expanse where the birds fly (Jeremiah 4:25), this is the atmosphere we live in, the celestial or 2nd Heaven is where the sun, moon and stars are (Genesis 22:17), and the 3rd heaven is where God makes his abode, the Apostle Paul refers to this in 2 Corinthians 12:2-4.

The lower or denser (thick) air (Heaven) is the second Heaven!

This is referred to in our vernacular as outer space! Its atmosphere is a vacuum. There is no oxygen or air, meaning the air is dense! To reside there, you would have to be in a shuttle or a spacesuit to supply you with oxygen!

Outer space is 100 km above the earth, 62 miles straight up! For a space shuttle it takes 150 seconds to reach the 2nd Heaven, where the stars reside! The earth has a shell of air that surrounds it, that sustains us with oxygen which we need, and our entire atmosphere is held in place by gravity! My God is incredible! This is the place the Lord Jesus took me to (in the spirit realm) to show me what the enemy was doing!

We know Satan has allocated power because the scripture tells us so.

In 2 Corinthians 4:4- *"In whom the god of this world hath blinded the minds of them which believe not."*

The Apostle Paul refers to him as "god of this world".

Jesus also said in John 14:30- "*I will no longer talk much with you, for the ruler of this world is coming, and he has nothing in Me.*"

Jesus refers to him as the ruler of this world.

But even so, we still have all power over the power of the enemy!

In the world today 235 million people have been diagnosed with the chronic disease "Asthma."

Asthma is a respiratory condition marked by spasms in the bronchi of the lungs, causing difficulty in breathing. It usually results from an allergic reaction or other forms of hypersensitivity.

It's a lack of airflow caused by blocked airways to the lungs.

Attacks can be triggered by anything from cold air to mold, mildew, dust mites, pet dander, anger, fear and stress!

The variety of triggers alone, from something physical to something emotional, helped me to realize that if there are emotions affecting the physical, there's almost always something in the spirit realm operating! By the finger of God, we have seen many healed of asthma by commanding the spirit to go in the name of Jesus!

While dealing in deliverance, demonic spirits will be expelled through sneezing, coughing, flatulence, gagging or simply a sigh! These are all ways of exhaling or expiration naturally! They will come out in like manner! Remember the Greek name for spirits is "Pneuma" meaning air!

Once my grandson, Jeremiah, was in the hospital with pneumonia! The Lord told me to command the spirit behind it to go. When I did, it left him instantly, and he was healed of pneumonia!

The enemy will use the air around us to kill, steal and destroy us!

With this being said: take authority over the air that surrounds you!

Matthew 18; 19 says – *"Again I say unto you, that if two of you shall agree on earth as touching (about) anything that they shall ask, it shall be done for them of my father which is in heaven."*

Let "us two" agree in prayer…

Father, we come to you in the name of Jesus, knowing you are God! We repent for anything we've done knowingly and ask you to forgive our shortcomings! We confess our faults Lord, as your children, you said if we did, you are faithful and just to forgive us. We take authority over the atmosphere that surrounds us, commanding all contaminates and toxic pollutants to diminish and dissolve even as we speak! Every plot and plan of the enemy and his use of the air, and his fiery darts, be consumed by our shield of faith. We destroy you with the Sword of the Spirit, no longer will any weapon you formed prosper! ! Any damage done by the enemy in the air, from asthma, sinuses, sarcoidosis, Covid-19, COPD, pneumonia, lung cancer, and any respiratory dysfunction,

We command healing from our head to toe, that you have provided on Calvary's cross! Applying every stripe, we were healed, and we receive it now, in the name of Jesus Christ!

We prophesy to the wind, the breath of the Lord, as it passes through our airways to fill our lungs afresh! We breathe in your Spirit, Lord, and speak life to every cell and tissue, every organ, vein, and artery, our blood and every bone in our physical bodies, that they will live and regenerate anew, in Jesus name! Now! And I thank you, Lord, for my healing!

There is warfare in the air!
But he sent his word, and they were healed!
Now breathe!

18

Angels watching over us!

We could never talk about the spirit realm and not speak about God's mighty angels!

Jesus reminded us he could have called down legions of angels while he was on the cross...but he didn't! This he did for our sake! He endured the cross!

As a pastor, I would always look at some of the errors of mankind and be confused as to why we do some of the things we do! Notice I said we, because I have definitely made my share of mistakes.

Since I did not grow up in the church, I really wasn't aware of how things were done as a leader in regard to protocol. I had so many that would say "You need an armor bearer" or would want to be an armor bearer to help assist me in some of my pastoral duties.

But I was always so repulsed by the abuse that I had witnessed in the church in this area!

People were used like slaves running around for some of these leaders, who would not serve, only want to be served! They would wipe the sweat off of the brow of their pastor, or dress them, or clean their houses, wash their cars, ridiculous stuff, in the name of the Lord!

In the Bible, the armor-bearer carried the weapons of his king or commander (Judges 9:54). In today's church, this nonsense has gotten out of hand! Many walk by titles, not function. The Lord named the function, an office: apostle, prophet, pastor, teacher, evangelist, but man wears it as a title, with no fruit following! In biblical times, when a prophet came to town, everyone knew he was commissioned by God to speak forth the oracles of God! This was his function. Just a sidebar pointing to my disdain for lunacy!

When I was ordained as a pastor, then commissioned as an apostle, I told no one for two years. It was such a bad taste in my mouth the amount of abuse in the church. The Lord spoke to me, and he told me not to throw the "baby out with the bathwater"--just obey and serve him the way he wants me to and he would help me to walk this call out! He prearranged the function. Satan just perverts it, and man is who he uses!

One day, while sitting in my office, the Lord told me, "Your armor bearer is my angel and you have five weapons in your arsenal."

I literally could not move! What a powerful revelation as to how the Lord showed me his way in this matter! I saw the angel at that moment. He had a quiver (a container for arrows) and it had five arrows in it or five spiritual weapons!

The word armor-bearer in the Hebrew is "Nasa"! This word means "able to bear up, lift up, carry, to help, or advance," just to name a few! The Lord reminded me about the angels,

"For he shall give his angels charge over thee, to keep thee in all thy ways. They shall bear thee up in their hands, lest thou dash thy foot against a stone (Psalms 91:11-12)!!

"The weapons of our warfare are not carnal," he was showing me, in the Spirit realm who was actually carrying the weapons (his angels) and how many weapons were in my arsenal!

I could not speak after seeing this vision! I see it even now! This revelation made a lot of sense to me! If our weapons were not carnal, then surely an armor-bearer, or human being would not carry them! Our weapons are mighty through God to the pulling down of strongholds!! The fight is also not against flesh and blood, but principalities and powers, wickedness in high places!

Remember, *Isaiah 54:17 says, no weapon (artillery, tools, vessels) formed against you shall prosper;* the enemy has weapons, but so does the Lord! This is good news for those who engage in the warfare of the Lord!

God's Angel is my armor-bearer! Who else could *"bear me up" lest I dash my foot against a stone"* *(Psalm 91:12).*

What many are calling an armor-bearer in the church today is really a deacon or a minister. I'm not causing a fight; this is just the way the Lord gave it to me.

I thank God for his angels! They have always helped me! I know this sounds different to some of you, but stay close to the Lord, and you will soon see I'm speaking in truth!

God's angels are mighty in War!

Once, while preparing to speak at a conference, as I walked to the podium, I saw the angels, with swords drawn, and lightning flashing, and the sound of thunder tearing through the room! Before I opened my mouth! I looked at all that was going on around me in the Spirit realm, smiled, and watched the Holy Spirit move in signs, wonders, and miracles all through the meeting!

All I did was watch the angels move on the Word of God as I spoke it!!!

Demons were manifesting and being cast out all over the room, healings were coming forward, the power of God, and his angels at work were a sight to see! I am always in awe of the Lord!

Man would love to take credit for what God has done, but this would be an absurdity! It is humbling to witness his power and presence at work in our midst!

In the earlier years of my ministry I would ask the Lord to show me his angels! I want to see them! I don't want to imagine; I want to see them!

I worked in the travel industry for 27 years of my life. One day, after getting off work I was walking to the elevator of the building I worked in. The Lord showed me I had an angel on each side of me, with one standing in back of me. For some reason they were walking in step with me! The Lord was showing me how they watched over my every move!

I taught a Bible study during that time, at the Department of Defense incognito, and we had signs, wonders and miracles happening on a regular basis there! In the conference rooms, on the stairwells, in the bathrooms, in my office, wherever the Spirit of the

Lord was, there was liberty!!

The angels of the Lord would always show up, ministering, protecting, encouraging, and strengthening me with whatever the Lord instructed me to do!!

His angels would wake me in the morning to pray, or help me through my fast, or remind me they were there in the battle! The Lord's angels are his host, or army, that truly has taken care and protected me!

I asked the Lord to show me his angels, and he frequently does, by his Holy Spirit!

While at lunch with a young lady one day, we were talking about her sister who was very ill. At that moment the Lord showed me his angels, one on each side of her sister, soaring up to the heavens. I told her she needed to go home right then! Later we discovered her sister went on to be with the Lord at that moment! But I saw the angels all around her escorting her!

We are not alone, even when we depart from this earth!

Even when the Lord comes, the angels will gather us from the four corners of the earth, (Mark 13:27)!!

The angels, God's angels, his messengers, and his army, are a force to be reckoned with.

The scripture says: ***"For He will give His angels charge concerning you, to guard you in all your ways" (Psalms 91:11)!***

Preceding engagements to minister the Word I was made aware of their presence. While at the same time, I'm sure there are countless times they have ministered to me, and I was not aware!

I can recall when I was a younger lady in my twenties; I was a new believer in Jesus Christ, trying my best to what new believers do.

On a beautiful, sunny day, I had an encounter.

I was attending a crab feast on the East Coast. Eating blue crabs is a way of life for many in the summertime! Friends and family would come together, crack crab, and have a good ole time!

On this particular Saturday, the feast would be at my house. I went into our local seafood diner to place my order.

You would go to the counter, order your food, and wait until your number was called, signifying that your order was ready.

While I was waiting, a gentleman came up to me and started a conversation. He was very subtle in his approach. He talked about the weather, how good it was, then, carefully, started to talk about God and his goodness! Before I knew it, he was telling me how the Lord would use me for his people and this light he placed in me would shine on God's people. In the midst of him speaking, I began to notice that in spite of the people all around us, I could only hear his voice! The area we were standing in seemed lit up, like a light was shining down into our conversation!

He encouraged me to go forward in the Lord and I felt a peace with every word he spoke! Finally, my order was ready. He waited for me to get my order, told me to "take care" and walked toward the door in front of me. He never ordered!

As he pushed the door open to leave, I caught it, and he was gone! I was close enough behind him to see the back of his head and touch him, but when he exited the door, he disappeared right before my eyes! I could not move. Looking all around, the only thing in front of us was the parking lot! He stepped out of that door, right back into the spirit realm. I sat in my car in that parking lot for a minute in absolute amazement, and I thanked God for sending his angel to minister to me!

Be not forgetful to entertain strangers: for thereby some have entertained angels unawares" (Hebrews 13:2).

While in service, I have witnessed angels pouring oil over me before I would lay hands on someone! I have watched angels, at a minister's command, stop a young man from running into the street to kill himself, and put him down on the ground, so we could take hold of him and command the evil spirits to leave him!

"Are they not all ministering spirits, sent forth to minister for them who shall be heirs of salvation" (Hebrews 1:14).

I would pray and ask the Lord to place his angels all around my house, because of the warfare that I'd engage in. One evening, while praying in my room, I looked out the window to see hundreds of angels, brilliant and tall, all around my house! I shut the curtains instantly; I was overwhelmed, afraid, and breathless all at once! I had never seen anything like this! The Lord was faithful to me, he was protecting me, and he wanted me to know it!

I have seen his angels (by the Holy Spirit), going in front of me, worshipping in our services, protecting cars, airplanes, streets, houses, battling with demons, standing over churches, stopping my vehicle from crashing, and countless other incidents!

"Bless the LORD, you His angels, mighty in strength, who perform His word, obeying the voice of His word" (Psalm 103:20).

The Lord's angels are designed and fashioned to be a present help. They were here for our Lord Jesus Christ, after he was in the wilderness when the Devil tried to tempt him. And they are here for us as well!

"Then the Devil left Him, and angels came and ministered to him" (Matthew 4:11).

This is a perfect example of how the spirit realm works with the natural realm that we live in! The angels go back and forth at the Lord's command! I am so blessed to truly know God's angels as a help to the believer; I have experienced this on many occasions!

In Daniel 6: 22- Daniel said, *"My God hath sent his angel, and hath shut the lion's mouths."* God sent his angels from the spirit realm to fight this battle for Daniel in the "world we live in"!

He will do the same for you, and he does!

Lord, I thank you for your angels. Your host (your army) in times of war!

19

Tell them to go!!!!

An unforeseen grace on my life is deliverance.

When the Holy Spirit introduced me to the Spirit realm, I saw unclean, evil, demonic entities of all sizes, and I was overwhelmed with fear! I could not imagine that I would ever get past the fear I experienced at that time in my life! This was a big deal to me because this was an area the Lord would use me in while training me, all at the same time! I was learning about the demonic and contending with these entities simultaneously!!

Discerning of spirits is one of the gifts of the Holy Spirit, enabling you to see and hear good and evil in the spirit realm! This is what I call an eye-opening gift! But this proved to be crucial in becoming familiar with my surroundings!

After every deliverance session, I went home and these spirits tried to follow me, torment me, bruise me, and attack me!! Why would I ever want to continue in this ministry of deliverance and get a ***whooping*** afterwards! This felt like such a cruel introduction to "setting the captives free"!

In the beginning, the attacks from these evil spirits were against me! I couldn't see them, only smell, hear or encounter a fleshly attack in my body usually at night!

I used to wake up at night with bruises on my legs and arms on a regular basis! My skin is dark, so to have a purple bruise overnight meant something or someone was really trying to injure me physically!

I recall, on one occasion, I used to wear a gold cross around my neck that I slept with.

In the morning I'd wake up to the cross on the backside of my neck, and my back would be scarred from it. By the looks of the imprint it was scarring my back by moving in a back and forth motion! The area on my back would be torn and sore! I removed the cross, of course, knowing that this would solve the problem, and my back healed!

A few days later, I awakened to the same, but fresh scratches and scarring on my back. I had no cross on. The enemy wanted me to know he was responsible! My life was turned upside down!

The demons declare war at night!

I remember having a dream and realizing it wasn't a dream. I opened my eyes to the feeling of being choked while lying in my bed!! Suddenly, a voice said, "God does not give us the spirit of fear"!

Nevertheless, I was still being choked!

Finally, I saw a vision of me standing against a 10-foot-tall brown-skinned man with platform shoes on, wearing a burnt orange suit and his hair was in a huge Afro, straight out of the '70s! What on earth?

I couldn't believe all of this was happening! However, when this soul brother started to attack my grandfather (in the vision) I grabbed him by the hair and commanded him to leave in the name of Jesus!

Instantly, the choking stopped! And the giant man melted down to just an Afro in my hands!

This was 30 plus years ago, I was a babe in Christ, and all of this was new to me!

Two nights later, at 2:00 am, the Lord woke me and told me to go into the living room, He instructed me to not turn on the lights, but he would be with me! Of course, I pondered the idea. "Why can't I turn on the light, and why do you need to be with me? Lord, what's in the living room"? The moon was shining through the sliding glass doors and I could see sufficiently to distinguish everything in the room.

A family member was asleep on my couch, and over his head were two huge demonic spirits with a jet-black hue, likened to a mass of darkness!

One stood at the foot of his body and one at his head! They moved when I came into the room as if to gesture defensively!

I was a mother in a nightgown, and my kids were in the other room in their bunk beds!! What on earth was going on in my living room?

The Lord spoke, "Command them to go!"

What? These things are demonic and active! Fear started to overtake me but the Spirit of the Lord spoke again, "Tell them to go in the name of Jesus!"

First, I must have just said the name of Jesus ten times in fear! Just the appearance of this evil made me start to hurry back to my room!

Finally, the Holy Spirit said to me again, "Tell them to leave." I commanded them to GOOOOOOOO, and instantly they rushed out!! I could not believe this was happening in my living room!!! But this was just the beginning of my encounters with the spirit realm!

The Lord has been diligent in teaching my hands to war in this realm! I could have never imagined this or that He would have me train others to do the same.

On one occasion a young man came to me seeking deliverance. He could not control his behavior in some areas of his life, he felt out of control or compulsive in his actions! Anger was ruling him, and he was aware of a presence. If you were to meet this young man, he looks like he's thinking all the time.

Have you ever met individuals who exhibit delayed conversation, as If they are really processing what you're saying to them--that was his demeanor!

When I sat down to counsel him, he started to laugh, I asked him why he was laughing, and he advised me that all day and night he hears voices speaking to him and constant noise, but as soon as we were getting ready to address these spirits, the voices remained silent. He was shocked! There was silence in his head instantly. The demons were aware of the presence of the Holy Spirit, getting ready to address them, so they stopped talking!

This helped him to realize he was being tormented and was not observant to the constant noise in his head, until there was no noise!

The Lord delivered him of the voices, and he was

healed of an infectious disease, all at the same time!

When light exposes what's in the darkness, darkness must flee. But we cannot be afraid of the dark!

Remember this is war!

20

Demons in the closet

It is impossible to talk about the realm of the Spirit and not address demonic spirits. I have never had a greater desire to expose anything more than I do in this area! I have witnessed people in such torment and agony, needing to get free from this kind of bondage, yet not having any help or answers or instructions on what to do!

In 2006, my family had an encounter that forced my children to see life from a different perspective. It was a snow day. While I was at work, I got a call from my daughter Jahnae, "Ma, you won't believe what happened!"

While my three daughters and son were watching TV in our living room downstairs, they heard a noise coming from upstairs, and they decided to investigate! They all proceeded upstairs, following the trail to my bedroom closet! There were clothes in a plastic bag, (that I was collecting for a homeless drive) and they were being thrown out of the bag piece by piece all over this walk-in closet! There was no one in the closet! Yet while they watched, clothes were continually thrown out of that bag!! Needless to say, everyone ran, jumped, cascaded, down the stairs over the banister, out of that room, as quickly as humanly possible!

This continued until three bags were emptied all throughout the closet! Hence, demons in the closet!!

These sorts of manifestations were happening because I was operating in so much deliverance at our church and in the community. These spirits were trying to intimidate me to stop deliverance in the area! There were times when I had no choice but to contend with a demon!

My son, Christen, brought a homeless man home once to feed him. They were in the basement; I was upstairs taking a nap. The Holy Spirit told me to wake up, go downstairs, and to command that spirit out of my house! I didn't know who or what he was talking about, regarding my house, but as soon as I commanded it to leave, and went downstairs to investigate, he was running out of my house!

I have run a homeless feeding for at least 25 years now. This has always been a burden on my heart, and so this man being homeless would be an opportunity to serve, like my son was proceeding to do.

But the Lord was showing me that what the man brought with him demonically was entering my home, and I needed to run it out!

You cannot invite everyone into your house. When casting out demons, at times, the demons have tried to linger. Not today, and not in my house!

I have seen the supernatural in this area of angels and demons and the variety!

Some of the manifestations of demonic entities on this side of the realm have been too challenging to explain; here are a few examples:

I had a young lady from Pennsylvania come out to one of our schools seeking deliverance. She claimed to be nine months pregnant; to look at her it was extremely obvious. Her belly was very large and elongated! The remainder of her body was not overweight or out of proportion. She just looked very pregnant! Her grandmother brought her to the class. She was there for mental unrest, but no one told me she was pregnant until she arrived. As I spoke with her, the Holy Spirit gave me a "word of knowledge" informing me she was not pregnant, and it was a demonic spirit that made her look that way! I asked her grandmother if she had gone to the doctor--yes, she had and the doctor confirmed she was not pregnant. We prayed and rebuked the demon!

I prayed for a young lady who had been through years of abuse. As we commanded the spirit to come out, her entire face became the face of her abuser as the demon exited!

An animal spirit manifested in a young lady's body and her neck fanned out on both sides, her feet indented like paws, she started sniffing! Still, the Lord set her free that day! Animal manifestations are more pronounced these days!

Calling out palsy in a crowded room, the display would be instant twisted hands fingers, legs, neck and, crossed eyes!

An older man fell to the floor and sat like a frog, with his leg turned outward from his body as we commanded the evil spirits to leave in the name of Jesus!

While in a church service, I was commanding ruling spirits over a young lady to release her. Instantly a warning signal came over my phone, (my phone was dead by the way) announcing there was a tornado coming, take cover! The Lord advised me to continue in the deliverance. Instantly a tornado rose up outside the building upon the command to the demonic spirits to come out! My husband and another pastor went outside of the building and began to rebuke the winds until they ceased. The demonic hold was broken as we took authority over these ranking devils, and the young lady was "rent sore" with convulsions and contorting as they exited her body. Our car was one of the only ones in the parking lot that received damage! This sweet young lady had been exposed to much occult activity, including the worship of many demon gods. The ruling spirits involved were determined they would not free her, but the finger of God said otherwise!

The Lord commanded a demonic spirit to come out of a lady, dealing with a defiant will. As the spirit came out, a fly exited from her mouth in front of the congregation! Beelzebub, (Satan) is the Lord of flies, or the dung-god, and he wanted me to know this was his territory! But we have all authority through our Lord!

After a deliverance service, a young lady went to the restroom where worms were coming out into the commode.

And the manifestations go on and on!

I remember the Lord telling me before I rose up to speak in a pulpit: "You are standing under an open

Heaven (I really did not understand what that meant in those days). He gave me a specific 'Word" for this congregation. They were putting new wine in old wineskins. It was a judgment, a rebuke! After I merely told them what the Lord said, I went to take my seat. As I walked back to my seat, I saw the 3rd Heaven, literally, right above me! I was speechless. I continued to my seat and sat down. Instantly, everyone who walked under that open Heaven fell to the floor! There was just silence in the room! No one could even get to the pulpit because it was under the "open Heaven."

The realm of the spirit is eternal; we live in a temporary state of being! The sooner we take hold of this revelation, the better equipped we will be to fight in this invisible war!

21

This Flight was Trans-spiritual!

Sometimes I have a hard time watching the News! It's a depiction of the world spiraling out of control and submitting to the likes and the works of the Devil himself!

I am 58 years old, and I have never witnessed the things going on in our society to this magnitude! Everyone is seeking to be politically correct, not to offend, but having to compromise your basic moral values just to subsist, calling this a "new normal."

"Every man did that which was right in his own eyes" (Judges 21:25)!

I mentioned earlier I worked in the travel business for 27 years. Common knowledge in the industry is when a flight crossed over the Atlantic Ocean it was referred to as a "transatlantic flight." In this lies the inspiration for the title of this chapter.

Seventeen years ago, the Lord showed me how some things work in the spirit realm. This has now become truth to me.

One night, while lying down to sleep, the Lord visited me! The Holy Spirit stirred me to wake up! The Lord Jesus was telling me to come with him. I was in the Spirit, meaning I moved in the spirit realm with the Lord. We went into an area that some refer to as the second Heaven. The first heaven is the atmosphere that we live in; the second Heaven is where the stars reside.

The third Heaven is where the Lord sits on his throne, with Jesus on his right side (2 Corinthians 12:2-3)!

I only received a better understanding of this when I experienced this with the Lord personally!

As we were traveling, it was like moving without walking or any kind of restraint! I was speaking with the Lord, moving with ease and not concerned regarding where I was going!

This flight was Trans-spiritual! I crossed over to the realm of the Spirit!

When I look back on things of this nature, I am amazed that I am not afraid. I am with Jesus, and it feels very natural, as if this mode of moving with the Lord is comfortable to me!

I understand the scripture when it says, *"But the natural man receives not the things of the Spirit of God: for they are foolishness unto him: neither can he know them, because they are spiritually discerned" (1 Corinthians 2:14).*

One cannot wrap their natural mind around this!

It's not mental or natural. It's spiritual and supernatural! This is why we have to renew our minds (Ephesians 4:23)!

When we arrived in the second Heaven, there was total darkness all around the area we were in! The Lord was standing beside me and he told me to look in front of me!

There were nine women in front of me, it was dark all around them and they were sitting. I said to the Lord, "I see nine women." He said, "Look again."

This time, I saw nine women covered with demons! The Lord said, "I want you to pray with them." My response was "Ok, Lord," then the Lord escorted me back.

The next day I thought about what the Lord had showed me! I wasn't sure what would come next, but the Lord directs our paths! By the end of that week, nine women had called me and wanted a private deliverance. The Lord instructed me to pray for them as a group! As the session got started, the manifestations of demons were evident! The Lord confronted the enemy in my presence! That is the way I look at it. I was there watching the Holy Spirit handle demons of all sorts, and they obeyed the Lord's commands! They were cast out and went yelling and screaming!

There was one young lady; we will call her Rebecca, for the sake of privacy! She had been in a relationship with a young man of another faith! He had given her bracelets as a gift. After their relationship was over, she could not move forward!

She felt controlled by him and could not function! She gained weight and could not remove these bracelets! The Lord said to command the accursed thing to go now (Joshua 7:12-13)! An accursed thing is an object that has either been dedicated to an idol or is a doomed object that God wants destroyed!

The bracelets were an accursed thing, they had to be removed.

As I commanded the bracelets to come off and the spirit behind it to leave, she was thrown across the chairs in the room and the bracelets flew off of her wrist!

There are so many things in the spirit realm that we cannot see that will keep us tied-to or hold us in an undesirable situation! Not just the soul tie that Rebecca had with this person, but also the accursed thing, the bracelets, held her in a place of witchcraft, controlled by a demon that had orders to oppress her! Truly the Lord knows the way to freedom!

All nine of the ladies were set free!

There is one of the nine about whom I wanted to share with you. The experience points to our culture today!

There was a young lady who had been sexually abused growing up! Her adoptive mother was the abuser! Latrese was engaged and brought her fiancé with her to the deliverance! He was a skeptic. Even though he was a believer, walking with Christ, he believed a Christian could not have a demon, but he came to the session in support of his future bride.

This was a beautiful young lady, and her heart was yielded to the Lord; she just wanted help. She felt like when she would sleep at night, that something was having sexual relations with her!

She could literally feel this taking place but did not know how to stop these encounters! A lot of women have experienced this.

Again, this took place thirteen years ago! On plenty of occasions the Lord will have me to command a spirit out that I had never heard of! At that moment in the deliverance, I would just say what I hear the Holy Spirit speak, (by a word of knowledge) to get the person free and look up the demonic entity afterwards! I am always amazed at the wisdom of our Lord!! He is all knowing!

With Latrese, the Holy Spirit told me to call out a transgender Spirit! I really did not know what that was, but as always, I just commanded it to come out! The manifestation totally shocked me!

A physical, male organ started to protrude out of her pants! I have seen so many things in deliverance and I know the spirit realm is bountiful with demons, but this was my first encounter with this manifestation!

She was set free of that spirit as well as many others. Her fiancé was no longer a skeptic.

This really speaks to our society today in so many ways! Many people are struggling with their identity, based on what they feel! Be sensitive to what the enemy wants one to feel! They desire to bring confusion and force you to agree with them because you believe based on your feelings! It's understandable but your feelings can and will lie to you. Regardless of how we feel, God's word is the truth!

In war, one of the biggest weapons of the enemy is deception!

There's nothing new under the sun, and the Lord has given us all power and authority to contend with this fight, we just don't know whom we are really fighting! Even though the Word of God has made it clear, we keep looking elsewhere!

"For we wrestle not against flesh and blood, but against principalities, against powers, against the rulers of the darkness of this world, against spiritual wickedness in high places" **(Ephesians 6:12) This is truth!**

The Devil has always been a deceiver, it started in the Garden of Eden and he hasn't stopped yet!

God made male and female! The key word in this is **God**! He did the making! It wasn't based on culture or a social state of mind; it was God in his infinite wisdom designing you. You are still fearfully and wonderfully made (Psalm 139:14)!! The enemy is very strategic. He whispered to Eve, "You won't die if you eat the fruit" (Genesis 3:4)! Satan is the one challenging God. And he uses God's people to do it! Same ole devil, same ole tricks!

It's time to change your perspective; this is not a flesh and blood battle, but a spiritual conquest!

When you are walking with the Lord, it's not by way of the Atlantic, it's "by my Spirit says the Lord."

This war crosses dimensions, boundaries and realms!!

22

Teach me, Holy Spirit

I really don't even know where to begin with this chapter. I love the person of the Holy Spirit! Many don't perceive him (as a person) per se, but I do!

When people say, "God almighty," the Holy Spirit is the Almighty in the Almighty God! The muscle, the action, the verb!

I've learned so much from the Holy Spirit, and there's so much more to learn.

He speaks to my heart, from which the issues of life flow, to keep it pliable to the Lord.

Hebrews 3:7 - *"Wherefore, as the Holy Ghost saith, today if ye will hear his voice, harden not your hearts."* The Holy Spirit is commanding us to be open to hear, listen, and not be stubborn when he's speaking to our hearts!

God's Spirit has been here since the beginning.

Genesis 1:2 *"And the earth was without form, and void; and darkness was upon the face of the deep. And the Spirit of God moved upon the face of the waters.*

Where God is, surely his Spirit will be also!

The term "Spirit of God" comes from the Hebrew word "ruwach" which means wind or breath. The breath of God! The words "moved upon" mean to flutter or to hover. The picture or image here is the Spirit of God breathing over the waters, with a back and forth motion of inhaling and exhaling yet hovering!

In War, the Holy Spirit is a sustainer!!

God is Holy, his Spirit is Holy, henceforth, the Holy Spirit!

When Jesus spoke of the Holy Spirit he said, "***Nevertheless I tell you the truth; it is expedient for you that I go away; for if I go not away, the comforter will not come unto you; but if I depart, I will send him unto you"*** (John 15; 7).

The Word tells us that Jesus had to leave so that the Holy Spirit would come!

In the Bible, you will always see Jesus speak of the Father; and the Holy Spirit will speak of the Son! The Son will point you toward the Father; and the Holy Spirit will point you toward the son!

John 15:26 *"But when the comforter is come, whom I will send unto you from the Father, even the Spirit of Truth, which proceeded from the Father, he shall testify (bear record or report) of me."*

The Holy Spirit is the Witness of Jesus Christ! When we receive the Holy Spirit, we become witnesses also!

Acts 1:8 *"But ye shall receive power, after that the Holy Ghost is come upon you; and ye shall be witnesses unto me both in Jerusalem and in all Judaea, and in Samaria, and unto the uttermost part of the earth."*

WE ARE HIS WITNESSES!

This morning before I went back to writing this book, the Holy Spirit woke me up. Before I opened my eyes, he showed me an instant vision. I felt my heavenly language rising up on the inside and I began to speak in tongues. I got up and continued to pray in the Spirit, until there was nothing else to release into the atmosphere! While this was taking place, the Holy Spirit showed me visions of what he wanted me to pray for (pray about)!

Romans 8:26 says, *"Likewise the Spirit also helpeth our infirmities; for we know not what we should pray for as we ought, but the Spirit maketh intercession for us with groaning which cannot be uttered."*

This word "uttered' in the Greek means: to speak, to say, talk, and to utter words literally!

In the spirit realm this is so powerful, because we have what we say! One of the advantages when you are praying in tongues is you are speaking God's language in the earth, and it shall come to pass, because the Lord is speaking! You are speaking from the realm of the Spirit into this natural world! Heaven's will is being spoken in the earth! His will shall be done on earth as it is in Heaven!!

Ephesians 6:18 says, *"Praying always with all prayer and supplication in the Spirit and watching thereunto with all perseverance and supplication to all saints."*

How do you pray "in the Spirit"? Of course, it could only be by the Holy Spirit

with the language that the Lord has given through his Holy Spirit! This scripture is telling you to pray on all occasions using all kinds of prayers, with this in mind, being alert and always praying for the saints, that is, the believers!

This language is coming from my spirit where the Holy Spirit resides in me.

This can be done intentionally. I love this! What this means is, when someone asks you to pray for them, you can by faith, purposefully pray in tongues with them in mind. The Holy Spirit will lead and guide to ensure that you are lined up with the Word of God!

First Corinthians chapter 14:15 also tells us how this works in more detail. *"**What is it then? I will pray with my spirit, and I will also pray with the understanding."*** The word understanding speaks directly to the intellect or the mind and comes from another Greek word, "ginosko" which means, "to know."

Understanding is what I know for sure! These are facts that my mind and intellect comprehend! Facts are things you know to be true! For example, when I pray with my understanding, I know that the Lord loves me with an everlasting love. I know that it is his will that none of us perish. I know he will never leave me nor forsake me! This is the position we are to take when praying with our understanding.

This is very helpful when you have all kinds of thoughts roaming through your mind while praying! If these thoughts do not line up with what you know to be true (understand) about the Lord, it could be the enemy! These are the thoughts and imaginations you would place under obedience to Christ (2 Cor.10: 5)! **This is Warfare!**

This morning, when I woke speaking in my heavenly

language, I was binding and loosing. I was aware of what I was saying in the spirit because of interpretation of tongues, which is another manifestation of the Holy Spirit! As the Holy Spirit was praying through me, he was showing me pictures and images of people I knew, and people I did not know. He showed me things in a sequential order to be carried out in that precise manner.

This is what the Spirit was saying as I prayed, *"and I will give unto thee the keys of the kingdom of Heaven; and whatsoever thou shalt bind on earth will be bound in Heaven, and whatever you loose on earth will be loosed in heaven"* **Matthew 16:18.**

For instance, the Holy Spirit had me binding demonic spirits that were influencing a 15-year-old boy. I was interceding for something in his life about which I was not aware; but the Holy Spirit knows what he has need of. This is moving in the Kingdom, using the keys provided by the Holy Spirit. **Again, this is warfare**!

Notice;

God is a Spirit: and they who worship him must worship him in spirit and in truth (john 4: 24)!

This scripture teaches me first, God is a Spirit, not a man! And for those who worship him, which means to pay homage; to adore; to do reverence: it must be in the Spirit. This means with a mental disposition (decision) toward a spiritual life! Obedience to a life of truth (the Word) with the Lord being the truth!

You see, the way we reverence God is through this spiritual life we live and our attitude and obedience to his truth! This is what it means to be a disciple. And this is exactly what it means to worship in Spirit and truth. It's a lifestyle!

One of the things I have learned in this walk with the Lord, in the realm of the spirit is that the Holy Ghost is power!!! He is pure fire!!!

Since the Holy Ghost is holy (meaning, the most pure; the most consecrated; the most sacred) you can't go any higher than MOST!

When the enemy sees him in you, it provokes panic, terror, and certain unrest! The enemy doesn't know what your mission is! He doesn't know if you came to torment the demons before their time (Matthew 8:29). Demons can see Christ in you!

The Holy Spirit is also my instructor!

When I am faced with a challenge, first, I make my request known unto God. Next, I wait on the leading and the directing of the Holy Ghost. He may tell me, pray in tongues; turn down your plate and fast; read Psalm 91! Drink only water today, Lynne! Call your daughter and tell her to eat green leafy vegetables. Have one of the ministers give a sermon!! And the list goes on and on by the direction of the Holy Ghost!! He leads us into all truth and righteousness!!!

The Holy Ghost is your direct connect to God's wisdom, knowledge, righteousness, truth, healing, deliverance--whatever you stand in need of in the Kingdom!!

I don't know how anyone, any believer, walks this walk without the Holy Ghost! The Holy Spirit is the superintendent over the Church! The Lord sent him to take care of, to provide for, and to protect those he loves!

I love the Holy Ghost; he's everything to me!

Be filled with the Holy Spirit! He is "essential" in these times we live in!

The Holy Spirit is the power in this war!

23

Have Faith in God!

Now faith is the substance of things hoped for, the evidence of things not seen (Hebrews 11:1). It's hard to see faith without hope. You first must have "hope" to even reap the benefits of what faith can produce In the 'Realm of the Spirit" faith is like currency or money. When you use it, expect a return!

The Lord spoke to me one day, showing me there was something he wanted me to do. I was to rent a local clubhouse in a "not so attractive" part of town, set up tables and chairs, and cook a meal to accommodate at least 75 people.

The Lord was "starting something" with these instructions he had given me the motivation was his love! I could always feel his love for people. By faith the Lord was declaring war and delivering his people, recovering them from the strongholds of Satan and he wanted me to yield to his love for them!

Cooking has always been one of the ways I like to show love to individuals. But I was surprised the Lord wanted me to do such a venture for this venue.

At the time, I really wasn't aware of what I was doing; I was just following the leading of the Holy Spirit! I fasted and prayed, anointed my head with oil, and invited whomsoever would come. My faith (full reliance on Christ) was resting in the Lord.

This was his war!

I had no money for this, I worked a fulltime job doing the week, with four children, and at that time I was a single parent. My husband of 23 years decided to move to the Middle East and move on with his life. This ended in divorce. The stress level in my personal life was what I call "special"! I needed to be revived.

My situation felt hopeless, dead, and I just didn't know how to feel better! I could barely encourage my own children, because I needed encouragement myself. When you've believed God for every promise and you still come up empty-handed, what do you do?

I remember asking the Lord, "If you would only fix this part of my life first, Lord, then I could better serve you." But I have learned, his **will** be done, not mine! That's when he shows us, we are overcomers! How else will we learn we are overcomers unless we overcome?

The war does not stop for you to tie your shoes!

If you fall down and cry, the enemy will still shoot at you. You will learn how to run, with shoelaces flying, and trusting God to make it to the other side. We must have faith in God! Frankly, it doesn't matter how chaotic it appears to be. Have faith in God! Have faith in God! Have faith in God! This is the only resolve! Hallelujah!!

Let me take a detour for a minute and just encourage you!

The Lord's Word encouraged me! Don't stop moving, keep going forward! This is for those of you who have spent it all, can't get the breakthrough, don't know which way to go; PRESS FORWARD! Don't look back!! You barely escaped the pass! You couldn't even breathe back there. You cried back there! Pain, fear, worry and stress were all "Back there." You left with one shoe and one-word curses spoken over you! Back there! Let old things pass away!! THIS TOO SHALL PASS, IF YOU LET IT!!!

You're not alone, it may seem that way, but the truth is he never leaves nor has he forsaken you! Roll out of the bed, let your feet hit the floor, drop to your knees, and leave your old world right there. God is in your next move, and it is forward. The revelation of your old man will be the first fruit of the new you! Now, keep moving!

Let me get back on track:

For these services the Lord told me to cook. So I cooked for each service. Needless to say, I didn't know how to pace myself at first and my strength would be zapped after cooking! I was always fasting until the service was completely over. My energy initially would be depleted. If I went out of the state, I would get a hotel room that had facilities in the room to cook as well.

I've learned that when the Lord says to do a thing, and he gives the details, do it exactly the way he says to!

My spirit was willing, but my flesh was so weak,

and I still had to preach at these gatherings. My focus remained on the Lord and faith would be my shield, when the enemy started to murmur and complain in my thoughts. Satan and his demons are constantly trying to get us to forfeit the work of the Lord in our lives!

I did not have a plan; I just did whatever the Holy Spirit told me to do.

Now for those who don't know me, I have never been the kind of person who would be the first in line, or had to be the life of the party or wanted to be seen! I was not competitive, and I evaded ambition. I still don't understand ambitious folk!

Proverbs 19-21- *"Many are the plans in the mind of a man, but it is the purpose of the Lord that will stand."*

In those days I had very low self-esteem; I dealt with so much rejection in my life and felt extremely unattractive to say the least. I felt I had nothing to offer anyone. But I knew the Lord loved me, and I loved him! He was my strong tower that I would run to! Sometimes I hid in there!

Being obedient to him was all I had to offer, so I pressed on and did my very best to observe every detail the Lord was speaking!

In each service, if the Lord said, "Touch a forehead, I would touch the forehead. If he said, "Touch the feet, I would! Place your hand on the mouth; my hand went to the mouth. Whatever the Holy Spirit told me to do, I just did it!

My confidence was in the Lord only.

Now back then, I didn't know what a revival was; I did not call them revivals. I just invited people to come out and fellowship. By word of mouth, they started to come.

I'd preach a message from the Lord, and just yield to the Holy Spirit, and miracles, signs and wonders would follow! No one was more shocked than I! For two years straight I ran an ongoing revival from Virginia to Maryland and Washington DC.

The word revival means to return to life or to recover. The prefix to the word "re" means again or something that is being repeated! You lost something, or it "once was" and there was a regression. Only God can call a revival, and keep it going, and recover, restore and return to life something that has died!

The Lord will go in the midst of the war, in the midst of the "pandemic" and command healing, and life is restored! He's God, let's not forget who he is!!

The neighborhoods I went to were impoverished, disadvantaged and broken, producing people with similar calamities. From the stoplights to the cracks in the cement sidewalks, things were just hanging on by a thread. The Lord was bringing life and recovering his people in these areas!

Again, this is war!

When I simply obeyed the Lord's instruction, he moved among the people! He was teaching me the art of war in my obedience to him! This pushed me to follow his every lead. This opened me up to be used. I was in awe of his power and his love!

I never understood how anyone could take credit for something God has done. This is truly a sign of a deficiency for any person to feel responsible for a "move of God"! There are so many things that are impossible for humans, but with the Lord, it's a piece of cake!

The revivals restored God's people, but simultaneously, the Lord revived me!

I was a warrior lost in the war!

I forgot that the warrior in me never died. It just took a hit and was overcome by the cares of this world, until I realized the Lord had already overcome the world!

This was over twelve years ago, and the Lord has blessed me with a wonderful husband who has truly taught me what His love looks like. I am loved, and God gets all the glory!

We are merely clay! *But we have this treasure in jars of clay to show that this all-surpassing power is from God and not from us" (2 Corinthians 4:7).*

It's the treasure in the earthen vessel that distributes the power, not the clay!

I have learned in the trenches, *Have Faith in God; the Devil may start the war but our God will surely finish it!*

24

Heir of Authority!

Periodically, my husband and I drove to a well known tourist area in Virginia called Luray Caverns. This area is part of the beautiful Shenandoah Mountains. When you drive up the mountains, the roads are winding and it's known for accidents because of its elevation and sharp turns!

On one occasion, clouds covered the mountains, and the fog was so thick, it obscured our vision. Looking through the windows of the car you couldn't see outside! To the right of the car was the mountain; to the left of the car was a merciless cliff! Because of this fog, we had to stop in our tracks...on a curve! We just could not see!

The Lord instructed me to command the fog to move. So, I did.

Literally, instantly, it started to back up, until all the fog disappeared as we drove onward and upward.

The fog responded to the command of the Lord! The spirit realm affecting (impacting), the natural realm!

We have authority over the fog, in the name of Jesus.

The Lord showed me that he made fog! He created it. If the creator tells me to tell a part of his creation to move, it has to obey, because it is still him (God) that is saying it.

In this war, the enemy can use the natural elements!
From rain, to storms, tornados, earthquakes, tsunamis to mudslides, Satan loves stirring up the elements!

But thanks be to God, he made the wind and the rain, the earth and the mud and he's given us all power and authority over all the power of the enemy (Luke 10; 19).

I've commanded rain to stop, storms and even a tornado in our back yard, and they obeyed the Lord's commands. I truly believe the Lord can use every believer if only they believe. Faith believes the unbelievable!

For verily I say unto you, That whosoever shall say unto this mountain, Be thou removed, and be thou cast into the sea; and shall not doubt in his heart, but shall believe that those things which he saith shall come to pass; he shall have whatsoever he saith (Mark 11:23).

This scripture says so much to me. In order to believe God for anything, we cannot doubt in our heart. The more we exercise our authority in the spiritual realm the manifestation will start to appear in the natural realm!

Doubting is dangerous! Sometimes you may not get a second chance to believe God for something. You might have to exercise your faith instantly, at the drop of a dime, with a twinkling of an eye!

When I exercise my authority, I will acknowledge that the Lord is in me and I in him.

When I open my mouth to speak, I say my words intentionally; knowing the words are going to do exactly what God said they would do!

If I find myself doubting, I repent for not trusting God. All things are possible through Christ, but if I start to think of my own frailties I will stumble and fall!

I know what I am without the Lord; I can do nothing of myself. My source is Jesus! We must be connected to the vine, and realize we are an extension--a branch, not the main source. We lose our authority when we try to operate apart from the vine (**as a branch cannot bear fruit of itself John 15: 4**).

Moving in our flesh, commanding the Devil, screaming out of your flesh, you will still be devoured. We must stay connected to the vine, Jesus Christ!

Authority is the power or right to give orders, make decisions and enforce obedience. The biblical meaning Is privilege, the force to delegate influence!

God gives this authority to us! Apart from him, you're acting alone. With authority, you must have faith in the one who has allocated it to you. You are an heir of the King, meaning a partaker of his promises (Ephesians 3:6). We are a legacy of Jesus the Christ, the anointed one. With this inheritance we have received all authority over the power of the enemy!

This authority is God-given to his children.

The Lord has given us authority in this war!!

I have witnessed so many demons become enraged and fearful at the same time when I use the name of Jesus!

They yell, "Stop using that name!" Others literally tremble at the name! In the Spirit realm, the name of Jesus is ferocious, intense, pulverizing! Again, if I haven't expressed this earlier in this book, the name of Jesus is relentless to the enemy. His name has protected me from giants! It will send evil spirits hurling into outer darkness at lightning speed! His name shakes the enemy's foundation to the core and removes the spirit of fear, causing it to turn, tuck its tail, stumble and fall. The name of Jesus is the only name by which men can be saved! The power is in the name. Your authority is in the name! Jesus is the name!

Now let's exercise your senses (Heb. 5:14):

Close your eyes. Now say the name of Jesus. This time say it with authority! Keep saying his name! Now when you say it, see fire shooting forth as you say his name! Jesus! See this fire consuming every plot and plan of the enemy against your life!

Say his name, and see this fire breaking through every demon that stands in its path! You are using the authority of "the Name of Jesus" moving in the realm of the spirit, and shutting down the enemy!

When you wake up each morning, say out loud, "There's power in the name of Jesus!" In the middle of the day, say it again. Proclaim this again and again and again, until it is like breathing to you!

Therefore God has highly exalted him and bestowed on him the name that is above every name, so that at the name of Jesus every knee should bow, in heaven and on earth and under the earth, and every tongue confess that Jesus Christ is Lord, to the glory of God the Father (Philippians 2; 9-11).

Speak the Word; declare the Word. In this war, the enemy hates to be reminded of the Word! When the

Word became flesh (John 1: 14), and dwelt among them you become aware that the word is Jesus! The enemy knows Jesus came to destroy the works of the Devil (1John3:8). When you speak the Word, Jesus is destroying him all over again!!

Jesus put every power and principality to an open shame, disarming them and triumphing over them in it (Colossians 2; 15). This being the case, you understand why the demons tremble at his name, and they scream in anguish when we say it!!

Even the devils are subject to us through thy name (Luke 10: 17)

Say the name, call on his name, trust in the name, post his name, and proclaim his name!

Announce it to the atmosphere, to all who are listening, that "Jesus is Lord of all!!

This is War!!!!

25

Warfare!!

Warfare! I hear this term used constantly all through the churches! Mentally, everyone has his or her own interpretation! Books are written about it. But I believe the best commentary for the Bible, is the Bible. What does the scripture say about warfare?

In II Corinthians 10: 3-6- *"For though we walk in the flesh, we do not war after the flesh; For the weapons of our warfare are not carnal, but mighty through God to the pulling down of strongholds; casting down imaginations, and every high thing that exalteth itself against the knowledge of God, and bringing into captivity every thought to the obedience of Christ; and having in a readiness to revenge all disobedience, when your obedience is fulfilled."*

The term "warfare" comes from a Greek word, "strateia." The biblical meaning is military service, apostolic career, as one of hardship and danger. Spiritual warfare tells you that you are in a battle; it's not with flesh. This is a war taking place in the realm of the Spirit. The weapons you use are not man-made and

God supplies the armor! It's a fight of **faith;** your enemy is not wrapped in flesh, but spirit!

Most people really don't believe there are evil spirits or demons, demonic influence, or that a spirit world really exists.

Even Christians who have a Bible, the Word, which is a witness to these truths, are still unclear in their stance, or disregard the Spirit realm altogether! Therefore they are never engaged! Meanwhile the Enemy is throwing darts, and slander, and sickness and disease, wreaking havoc on you and your family and you are still praying for God to do something, whereas the Lord is trying to get you to put on the whole armor and fight!

Howbeit, we can believe in a God that is a Spirit, but not the Spirit realm where his throne abides!

We call him King yet do not acknowledge his kingdom. Again, what King does not have a kingdom, his domain?

If we are going to believe, we truly must believe! Do you believe?

When I came to the realization that evil does exist, and there really is a Devil, and demons do his bidding, I knew I needed the Holy Spirit to teach me more about my opponent. When I read the scriptures concerning the enemy, powers, principalities, rulers, thrones, dominions and the such, I didn't have enough understanding to withstand the attacks!

Warfare 101

Sometimes the Lord will put you into the fire--naked but covered!

I recall the Lord telling me to start a neighborhood

Bible study when I was in my 20s! I asked the Lord who would come, where would I get people from?

Within minutes, a young lady knocked on my door and literally asked me, "Why don't you start a Bible-study in the complex?" (she was a young lady I would encourage from time to time). I perceived the Lord was speaking!

During this time in my life, we lived in the ghetto. There was heavy drug trafficking and there was a hustle going on from corner to corner. The Lord will put light in dark places because God has a purpose. Yet while it's going on, it just feels like you're living in the ghetto!

To start the Bible study, I would fast all the time and follow the instructions of the Holy Spirit. Fasting for me was only drinking water, reading the Word, anointing my head while going to work, at a regular 9 to 5 job.

In those days, my children were small, and time seemed to move so fast. The Lord will give you a lot to do when you already have a lot to do, but he's just preparing you for more to come!

The Lord told me to anoint with oil the head of my front door. With this, no demon could enter unless I invited it. What on earth? Why would the Lord say this to me, I would never invite a demon into my House! I was petrified at the idea of it! But, being obedient, I anointed the top or the head of my door!

A week later I started the Bible study. On the first day it was about ten people in the neighborhood that showed up. The last person to show up was stand-ing outside my door, not moving. She advised me she wanted to come into the Bible study, but she couldn't cross over the doorpost. The Lord reminded me no demon could enter unless I allowed him to! Now, the Lord was saying to allow her to come in, so I did.

I opened the Bible study with prayer. As soon as I started to speak the Lord told me to command the evil spirit in the lady to come out! I was brand new in uncharted water when it came to demon spirits! But I did what the Holy Spirit said to do, and she began to vomit!

In Mark 1:26- *"**And when the unclean spirit had torn him, and cried with a loud voice, he came out of him.**"*

The Holy Spirit taught me later that when a spirit is departing or being evicted, the tearing apart will manifest in the natural by someone vomiting or convulsing or something as simple as just releasing air.

This was the first time I had ever been moved by the Holy Spirit to this extent! In that very moment you are taking the fight to the unclean spirit in the spirit realm. Yet the manifestation was in the natural!

The Lord showed me, this is warfare!

Again, this was engaging in military service and it is the apostolic career, meaning one of hardship and danger, hence the definition of warfare!

The Church is apostolic by nature, Christ is the chief apostle, and this is his church.

This is letting you know, you have a military career in the spirit realm! You have been drafted, or better still engrafted, by way of adoption through Jesus the Christ!

Your commander and chief, Jesus, came to destroy the works of the enemy.

That tells you, since the enemy is still here, we do like our daddy did! Continue, by the Lord living in us, to destroy the works of the adversary!

In this war, we have to know how to stand! The Word promises the way to stand, first, is to put on the whole armor of God.

This means you have to make a conscious decision to do this. Put it on! You're not sleeping in this armor overnight, that's why you have to "put it on"!

This also tells you, you need to wear all of it. The whole (full) armor! One piece of armor complements the other piece. You can't do this half-dressed!

This fight promises to be different than the ones you may have experienced in your flesh. There's no need for name-calling, unless it is the Name of Jesus!

How do we fight this invisible battle?

Ephesians 6; 13-18 says "Wherefore take unto you the whole armour of God, that ye may be able to withstand in the evil day, and having done all, to stand. Stand therefore, having your loins girt about with truth, and having on the breastplate of righteousness; And your feet shod with the preparation of the gospel of peace; Above all, taking the shield of faith, wherewith ye shall be able to quench all the fiery darts of the wicked. And take the helmet of salvation, and the sword of the Spirit, which is the word of God: Praying always with all prayer and supplication in the Spirit, and watching thereunto with all perseverance and supplication for all saints;

In this fight truth is to be wrapped around your loins (the lower part of the back), like a belt. Truth helps us to stand upright! Whether you're twisted or bent to the right or to the left, (in this stand) Truth must be the belt worn for your support! This is not just a defensive posture, but one on the offense, as well, yet held in place by the truth!

John 14: 6-" Jesus saith unto him, I am the way, the truth and the life!"

A breastplate of the righteousness of Jesus protects all that is vital. This is so we will not look to our own righteousness, which is of no value to the "born again" believer!

This helps us to only go the way the Lord tells us to. Our righteousness allows us to justify our positions even when we are wrong. This is self-righteousness, and this will only benefit you.

To shod (to bind) your feet to this good news is the great commission with a readiness! We must be prepared to carry this message of reconciliation with God to man to a hopeless world!

A shield that has Faith stands and quenches whatever the enemy throws our way! This shield (in biblical times) was like a door you could hide behind. The fiery darts are arrows the enemy would send to ignite anger or lust, grief, fear, or torment, to name a few! This shield of faith is a reminder that salvation was provided for you already. You are saved; now believe it and don't accept what the enemy is throwing at you! Extinguish it with your reliance and belief in what Christ has done for us and what he says about you. You are more than a conqueror. You are healed, you are brand new, and old things really have passed away!

In this war we need the helmet of salvation rooted in Hope. This hope is a reminder that we are children of God! This protects our thoughts, our mind, and our will. Trusting in our salvation (deliverance) through Christ, we can know that we are saved! Keep this helmet in place by meditating on the Word over and over again, forming a mindset that is reliant on our Savior!

The Sword of the Spirit, which is the "Word of God," is a brutal weapon in our stand against the wiles of the Devil! This portrays the Word as a powerful weapon to contend with; because the tongue can be a deadly poison and able to set on fire the course of nature (James 3). It's imperative we use it with great caution! Speak the Word of God in this stand; it is alive and active (Hebrews 4; 12).

This is the "Word" in war!!!

The image of the armor is to withstand, to oppose, and to resist the enemy in this war with Truth, righteousness, peace, faith, salvation, and the Word of God!

Again, put on the whole armor of God. Rather, clothe yourselves with the Lord Jesus Christ **(Romans 13: 14).**

Now that you're dressed, you are suited and ready for war!!

26

Fight til The End

The Bible has always been a book of love, hope, encouragement, instruction, and truth!

My reminder to you is that Heaven will one day be our home. Yet while we are here, we have work to do! We have to be about our father's business, doing the work of the kingdom. The scripture teaches us that we only know in part, we see through a glass dimly, but one day we will know the Lord face to face. Until then, there is a spiritual world all around us that we cannot ignore!

The Holy Spirit is our guide, allow him to reveal what's hiding in the darkness, what direction the wind blows, when to bind and loose, when to wage war and when to pray, how to recognize the signs of our times, and how to stand lest we fall!

"This know also, that in the last days perilous times shall come.

For men shall be lovers of their own selves, covetous, boasters, proud, blasphemers, disobedient to parents, unthankful, unholy, without natural affection, trucebreakers, false accusers, incontinent, fierce, despisers of those that are good, Traitors, heady, high-minded, lovers of pleasures more than lovers of God;

Having a form of godliness but denying the power thereof: from such turn away" (2 Tim 3:1-5).

This scripture is referring to the Church, the "Body of Believers," in the last days! A sign of the times we live in will be evident in the church. These are perilous (dangerous and difficult) times; the description of the character of man is of one that is deceived!

They had a form of godliness or an appearance. The World doesn't try to look like the church. They are growing more and more intolerant of the church! This is the believer that is referenced. What will the church look like in the end?

Will there be any faith in the earth when the Lord returns? It looks hopeless, and "men's heart will fail", because of what some will experience, for the powers of Heaven will be shaken (Luke 21:26).

But he that shall endure unto the end, the same shall be saved (Matthew 24:13).

We must hold on to the hand of the Lord until our Lord returns. He has revealed to us his presence, his love, and his kingdom within us, exposing the darkness and demons in the closet, so fight til the end!

He has made us aware of the fight in the spirit realm and the angels that watch over us! He has told us we have power and has indoctrinated us with authority over "all the power of the enemy" by his name only! He reminds us that we are not fatherless children wandering aimlessly, abandoned and alone. So fight til the end!

His Holy Spirit leads and guides us in all truth, telling us we are more than conquerors and overcomers, all wrapped up in his armor. So fight!

We are not alone and, with him, there are more with us than the whole world against us! The Lord is inviting us to know him, to have a relationship with him today. Using intimate terms of endearment, calling us his children, beloved sons, and his bride, while expressing his love for us in so many ways. So fight til the end!

My dear friend, spend time in his Word, in prayer, and fasting. Be that doer of the Word, walk the Word out! In time, you will come to the realization that our God, he really is God!

In closing, I am perpetually grateful because the Lord has prepared a place for me eternally. I'm not just staying over; I have somewhere to go after the final trumpet call!

Thank you, Holy Spirit, for teaching our hands to war in the spirit realm, in combat with invisible enemies! Thank you for enabling us to see the unseen, fighting a war in the trenches, on our knees in our living rooms!

Jesus, I declare you are King! One day I will meet you in the air, the Lord, God almighty, sitting on his throne! Me, dressed in my incorruptible attire, in the realm of the Spirit where those who believe will all one day call home!

Soon we will fight no more, but for now, this is WAR!

CPSIA information can be obtained
at www.ICGtesting.com
Printed in the USA
LVHW041201171120
671900LV00006B/449